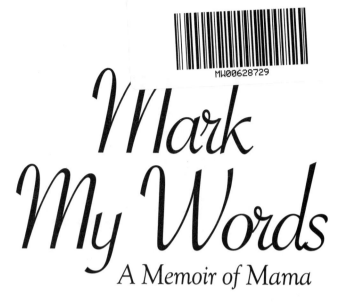

Mark My Words

A Memoir of Mama

Other Books by Ronda Rich

What Southern Women Know (That Every Woman Should)

My Life In the Pits (A Racing Memoir)

What Southern Women Know About Flirting

The Town That Came A-Courtin' (a novel and a movie)

What Southern Women Know About Faith

There's A Better Day A-Comin'

Mark My Words

A Memoir of Mama

[signed: Best wishes, Ronda Rich]

RONDA RICH

National Best-selling Author

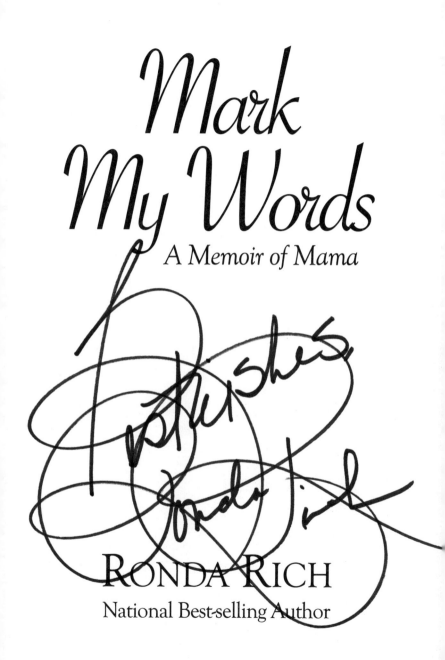

Published by Ronda Rich Creative, Inc.
P.O. Box 303
Clermont, GA 30527

ISBN 978-0-692-76010-9

Book and Cover design by Carroll Moore
Page 8 Photo by Kristen Mangum Cloud
Reprinted with permission from Kristen Mangum Cloud and the *White
County News*
Other photos including author photo by Selena Nix or from the author's
private collection.

www.rondarich.com

First Printing

Printed in the United States of America

To my niece, Nicole, who spent many joyful hours with Mama, eager to learn whatever she had to teach and, thus, helping to ensure that Mama's legacy will live on.

Our last Easter with Mama at the center of our family.

Life with Mama

When I introduced Mama to a fashion show with
400 women in attendance, they stood and cheered.
Mama was a star and she loved it. Twenty-six hours later,
the Lord called and Mama answered.

Mama

"Mark my words." I can hear Mama saying it now. It's a phrase I've picked up and I use whenever I'm making a prediction or declaration. So, this I can say: Mark my words. You're in for a treat with the stories that follow. Over the life of my storytelling, there has always been one character who was the most beloved and most popular because she was compelling and interesting. Mama told it the way she saw it even if it came at someone's expense.

One Sunday at church, Mama saw that one of her friends was suffering the misfortune of having gotten a bad home perm. It was frizzy and the ringlets were so tight that they clung to her head and laid flat. It wasn't a pretty sight 'a'tall' as sayeth our mountain kin. Most people would have been sympathetic but not Mama. When she saw her, Mama eyed her carefully and studied on her hair for a bit. I watched Mama watching her and girded myself for what was coming. Finally, she frowned, shook her head, leaned over to me and said loudly enough for those around us to hear, "Look at Eula Mae." Another shake of the head. "Do you think she has *any* idee just how *bad* she looks? If I'd been her, I'd stayed home. You can mark my words on that."

There were two signature sayings of Mama's. One was "Somethin' just told me." Mama had what the Bible refers to as discernment and prophesy. She could eye a situation and predict weeks, months or years down the road what would happen. Or she could see telling signs in people and situations and, out of the blue, declare unseen motives or a turn of events that no one suspected lay around the corner. "Somethin'" referred to a piece of discernment.

"Somethin' just told me," she would begin. This gift of Mama's was especially helpful whenever she lost things. She would look for it, without success, then go to her worn out blue recliner, sip on a cup of coffee and wait for "somethin'" to tell her where it was.

"It just come to me," she said once about some money she had misplaced, "to go and check the trash can in the pantry. I pulled out everything and there it was between a newspaper and magazine. I guess it was layin' on the table and I picked it up when I got them papers up to throw away. Somethin' just told me." I never knew Mama to lose anything permanently. She always found it, thanks to "somethin'."

Her other trademark phrase was "Mark my words." This she always used to illustrate a piece of prophecy. For us in the family, it was akin to the red letters in the Bible or whenever Jesus said, "Verily." We paid attention. Even if we did not like what she had to say.

"Mark my words," she said once when I was a teenager. "That boy is not what you think he is. You're going to rue the day you ever met him." It broke my heart that her words turned out to be true.

"Somethin' just told me," and "Mark my words" guided Mama – and those of us who had the treasure of knowing her – solidly through life's uncertainties and anchored us. Without the compass of those words, I would have made many more mistakes than the hundreds that I made because sometimes I was wise enough to listen. When Daddy died, we were all scared to face life without his powerful prayers. When Mama departed and took her "somethin'" with her, the foundation of our lives was thunderously rocked.

To the female readers of my newspaper column and books, we all sat together at the table of sisterhood with a kinship of understanding when it came to Mama stories. "Do we have the same Mama?" I heard often, or "We must be related because my mama is just like your mama." It was a thread of commonality woven through the fabric of my life that stitched it together with the lives of others.

Once I stopped by her house and asked as we ate supper, "Did you read my column this week?"

She nodded as she took a swig of buttermilk. Mama loved 'sweet' milk and buttermilk and drank both daily.

"What was it about?" I learned this trick from Daddy who would often ask us at the Sunday dinner table, "Whadda preacher preach about today?"

She didn't hesitate. "I don't remember." She took another sip of milk and swallowed. "It wasn't that interesting."

Though I wrote about Mama, unscripted and unfiltered, I always let Mama have the final zinger. For my readers, Mama had to win because, otherwise, it was sacrilegious. No one should take a sniper shot at motherhood. Even though she always had the upper hand, male readers were protective of Mama.

Johnny, a longtime friend who can say whatever he wants because he has confidence in our friendship, called to say, "You need to lay off your mama. You're too rough on her."

His brother, Bobby, also telephoned. "I tell you what – you never give your mama a break, do you?"

"I hope I live long enough to see you write somethin' good about me," Mama groused once in the early days of my column.

"I hope I live long enough to find somethin' good to write," I shot back and then laughed. Mama, to her credit, laughed, too.

"I'll work on mindin' my p's and q's," she replied with a cheerful smile. "I need to improve my public image." She winked.

Thank goodness she didn't. She was colorful, plain spoken, honest, compassionate when the need arose and very funny. Truth be told, that's one of the things that I missed the most after Jesus called her home: the quick-witted repartee that flew between us. But, almost always, the final word came from Mama. She was terrifically smart so she was hard to outwit and, definitely, to out-talk. When one of our repartees had ended because I had enough common sense to shut my mouth, Mama would look up, smile with joy dancing in her eyes, point her crooked forefinger in my direction and say, "Mama wins again. Don't get above your raisin' little girl and try to outsmart your mama."

A couple of summers before she died, we attended a Fourth of July cookout at my sister's house. Mama, at 85, was the only person older than 60 there with most of the folks being younger than 35. Someone had a chain puzzle with the links looped together. One by one, we younger ones all tried to solve it but, one by one, we each shrugged and gave up. After I had tried, I laid it down on a desk and walked away. Mama looked over, eyed it for a moment in the way that a toddler or puppy eyes something to grab, then quietly sauntered over to it. She picked it up and in less than a minute she untangled what a dozen people with younger minds and nimbler hands had been unable to do.

"Looky here," she said, holding it up and beaming proudly. A few laughed and bragged on her but most of us were stunned that we college-educated, successful professionals had been outwitted by a child of the mountains who had done her book learning in a small, one-room school house. And, she had done it in record time.

My friend, Karen, used to laugh at all the Mama stories I told. "You'd better hope your mama lives a long time," she said often. "Because when something happens to her, your career is over."

I worried that was true. But as Mama and the good Lord both would have it, once she crossed the River Jordan, I found a way to carry on. Both personally and professionally. Over the years that Mama has been gone, readers have often asked me to compile a book of stories and columns about Mama. Then one day, somethin' up and told me that I should do it. Just like it was my own idea. I discovered, as I began what was a more ardent task than I expected, that Mama had died four years after I started my syndication and while she was often mentioned in columns, the ones that were solely about her were less than 10 percent. It reminded me of the popular fictional character of "Ernest T. Bass" on *The Andy Griffith Show*. Ernest T. was so colorful, spirited and memorable that fans of the show always remember him as being a big part of the show when, in reality, he only appeared in five episodes. Mama is the Ernest T. Bass of my career. While she appears in only a small percentage of the stories I've told, she is the overshadowing figure who captivates and delights readers. She is the one who is remembered when all others are forgotten.

So, here's Mama. If you were already a fan of hers, you will be reminded of wonderful stories while finding some new ones written just for this book. In columns that are being reprinted, I have also added a bit of the inside story for each column. If you never met her or read about her, you're in for a treat. You're about to meet one of the South's most entertaining folks. When she died, a newspaper story about her began, "One of the South's greatest characters has died." Mama, a woman with unique language, viewpoints and smart insights, would have been proud to read those words and especially proud that it was a free obituary. Mama loved free. In the pages that follow, you will meet Mama at her glorious best. You have never encountered a more irrepressible, colorful, memorable character. Of that I can assure you.

Mark my words.

Mama Always Said

"Be careful what you tell your best friend because she may not always be your best friend. But she'll still know all your secrets."

Mama, Daddy and me on Mother's Day
(see our corsages) when I was four.

Widow Woman

*I*n the rural Southern mountains of my raising, a woman whose husband had died was always called "a widow woman." Churches and neighbors, following Biblical instructions, saw to it that these women and the orphans were fed and their earthly needs met.

Mama was 78 when she became a widow woman. Nine days earlier, she and Daddy had celebrated their 58th wedding anniversary. It is not with any disrespect to my daddy, whom Mama loved the moment she laid her eyes on him, that I say that the final 10 years of her life were her happiest and most joyous. He had been a solid provider even if the provided was lean at times and barely enough to go around. He was a Godly man who placed the Lord first and his family second so whatever it took to do right by the Lord and his family, Ralph Satterfield did it. He was a powerfully built man, with green eyes that could twinkle merrily or mist woefully over someone's sorrow or even darken angrily if crossed the wrong way, especially by a dishonest man. He stood tall at six feet, was broad-shouldered and never overweight. For all his life, his arms from the shirt sleeves down were a deep, roasted chestnut brown as were his face and neck from the farming and outside work he did. He owned a mechanic's garage, farmed the land and preached on Sundays at small Baptist churches in the mountains.

There is an irony in that.

Mama, raised in the Nimblewill Valley nestled in the mountains of Northeast Georgia, was the most popular girl in her community of the early 1930s, the years that our people would forever call "Hoover Days," named after the president that they believed put them in such a mess while the rest of the world knew it as the Great Depression. One county over, a long way in those days when most of the mountain folk were still traveling by mules and wagons, was the young man who would eventually win her heart completely. The other boys had been merely a teasing along the journey to her forever destiny. Bonelle Miller, slender, raven-haired, dark-eyed and blessed with creamy white skin and perfect teeth, was a daughter of the righteous. Her father, Ance, was a humble, good man who had a hard time providing for his family in a time fraught with heartaches and tribulations. His father-in-law had gifted them with a 40-acre farm, as he did with all his children, but it was lost when there wasn't enough money to pay the taxes during the darkest of those bleak Hoover Days. For the rest of their lives, they rented shack-like houses and land to farm collard greens and whatever they might sell or barter. For a half century, they would live at the mercy of landlords, always aware that they were just one month's rent away from being homeless.

Paw-paw Miller was also a spirit-called preacher, the calling he took with the utmost seriousness and reverence. In those days, churches in the mountains, outside of the towns, were all Baptist, owing to the fact that the Baptist ordain men called of the Holy Ghost, who aren't necessarily educated in theology. The mountains, bulging with Scotch-Irish, had been forced to forsake the Presbyterianism of their forebears because the Presbyterians ordain only well-educated men and those scholarly men did not cotton to the primitive living they found in those mountains. The Baptists, perhaps in the only way they have ever been liberal, were willing and eager to take men who studied faithfully the word of God and had been given the spiritual gift of discerning the scriptures of the King James Bible. Churches normally met one Sunday a month and shared a pastor with other churches.

Mama did not completely relish being a preacher's daughter, although she always admitted that she was proud of who her daddy was because the preacher and his family enjoyed something of an elevated standing in the community. Still, it could be challenging. The preacher's family was held to a higher standard and never allowed the privilege to stand up and defend their loved one when someone talked bad about the preacher. And, there were those dadgum white shirts that needed to be ironed and painstakingly starched in preparation for Sunday's service when the preacher would stand behind the rough-hewn, handmade pulpit to preach in the only dark suit and decent tie he owned.

"I tell you right now, I ain't never gonna marry a preacher," Mama promised as she slaved with an ancient iron over Paw-paw's shirts. "I'm not gonna have a life like this."

"Be mindful of what you say," Maw-maw warned. "You might have to eat them words."

Mama, always stubborn and often unreasonable when her mind was made up, continued harping against it, concluding, "I'm not. You just watch me. I ain't marryin' no preacher. No ma'am, I ain't."

Lizzie Miller, stick thin – poorly is what mountain folks called someone who needed fattening up because they were usually thin due to a lack of food and money – smoothed a wisp of light brown hair back from her forehead as she took a bobby pin from her bun then tucked it back in place and smiled. "I didn't marry no preacher neither." She paused. "But he made a preacher 'cause the Lord called him. You never know what the good Lord's gonna do, little girl."

Mama narrowed her eyes and straightened her shoulders. "You just watch me and see. You can mark my words on that."

True to her word, Bonelle Miller did not marry a preacher. She left those mountains when she was 18 and moved almost 50 miles away to Gainesville. She lived with her aunt and uncle, also mountain refugees, helping them in their boarding house while she also worked in the hosiery mill for 18 cents an hour and lived a far bigger life than she had known in the mountains. When it came down to choosing a husband between two ardent suitors, one a handsome, distinguished preacher and the other a saved-by-grace but secular man, she definitely stuck to her word. However, nine years and three children later, the Lord began calling the earnest young man. When His call wasn't answered readily, He called again. And again. Many were the times that His call was not answered. Still, He kept calling while Ralph Satterfield, a child of the renegade mountain folk (some of them moonshiners), ran with all his might. By the time God brought him to his knees, both Ralph and Bonelle were ready to heed to the Lord's calling and get all the trials and tribulations of their lives behind them.

"It was awful what we went through when Ralph was runnin' from the call to preach," Mama said. "I was to the end of my rope. There ain't no tellin' what would have happened if he hadn't give in when he did. I was just about crazy. I can tell you that."

When Daddy made a preacher, he fell into the arms of the Lord with an astounding mixture of humility and strength. Mama, with genuine gratefulness to the Lord, told of the night that Daddy had finally succumbed and met the Lord on the Lord's terms. It was during a church revival to which Maw-Maw invited him while Mama convalesced with a newborn at home. Maw-maw knew the terrible turmoil that was going on in their household and marriage. She was never intrusive into her children's affairs but she tried to always do as the Lord led her.

"Ralph, why don't you go to church with me tonight?" Maw-maw was visiting to help out with the children and planned to go to church with Ozelle, the oldest of her eight children.

"No, I don't think so," he replied. She said nothing but continued readying herself. In a moment, Daddy reappeared in the door and said, "Lizzie, if you'll press my suit for me, I'll polish my shoes and I'll go with you."

She smiled. "I sure will."

Aunt Ozelle told me many years later what she had witnessed that night when the preacher called for the sinners and those fallen from grace to come to the altar for repentance. Daddy wasted not a moment of time, falling onto his knees. "When he come up out of that altar, he was a changed man. I knowed, without a shadow of a doubt, that Ralph Satterfield had took hold of the mighty hand of God and would never let it go. And, he didn't. There never was a finer man once he set himself right with the Lord."

Over the years, whenever he knelt in a church to pray, he began often with "Lord, we humble our unworthy selves before thee." His strength in the Lord never waivered. Just as Aunt Ozelle had predicted. He wore out many a Bible – always King James, Scofield Editions and black ("out of the darkness came the light," he declared) – and knew the Word as deeply and profoundly as any well-educated minister. In fact, there were some scholarly preachers that he "learnt them a thing or two" as our mountain kin like to say. He was what is now referred to as 'bi-vocational,' meaning that he pastored churches for a love offering on Sundays yet worked by the sweat of his brow and the turn of his hand through the week to provide for his family. Once, he helped in a week-long revival with another preacher. When the offering plate was passed, a meager seven dollars was collected. Daddy gave it all to the other preacher. Like my mama's daddy, he, in the first half of his preaching life, served two mountain churches at the same time. One held services on the first and third Sundays while the other church met on the second and fourth Sundays. There was even a period when he pastored four one-time-a-month churches at once. When I was nine, one of those churches would go full-time to weekly services, so Daddy lived out his life as the pastor of one mountain church. He is buried in the graveyard of that church with a plaque that identifies him as a World War II veteran and the church's pastor for 34 years. He served God, country and family. A life can offer nothing better than that.

Mama, the one who had declared with absolute conviction that she would never be a preacher's wife, became one of the finest that the Appalachian foothills had ever seen. She was by his side for every service, revival, funeral or wedding. For much of his life, Daddy had revival meeting for three or four weeks in a summer since he pastored two churches and was often called on to help other pastors at their revivals. These were morning and evening services which extracted a mighty physical price, but rarely did Mama allow him to go without her. Over the decades, she probably missed no more than a dozen times and then it was because that either she or a child was sick.

"Honey, let me tell you this," she would say while counseling a young preacher's wife. "God didn't just call him. He called you, too."

With Mama firmly by his side, he visited the sick, preached to the living, married the sane as well as the foolish, baptized the saved and buried the dead. It was 1968 and he had been preaching for almost 20 years before he officiated at his first church wedding. Normally, couples just called and asked to come to our house to be married. When Mama heard that there was a wedding to be held, she bustled around, gathering roses from her glorious climbing bushes if the season permitted, baked a three-layer, white frosted cake and made coffee to celebrate. Her name signed as a witness to the uniting of a man and wife was affixed to many a marriage certificate which were normally signed on the kitchen table.

Mama, typical of our Scotch-Irish heritage, could be set in her ways and ornery. "Bull-headed," Daddy would say. But never once in the 36 years that I knew her as a preacher's wife did I hear her complain about the weight or the frequency of her duties. Sometimes at the end of a summer's week-long revival after 14 services, she might drop into her favorite chair, prop her feet on a stool and say, "I'm plum give out. But wasn't it good to see the lost saved and that Zora can still get Ezra to church once a year?" Sometimes, Daddy would do two revivals back-to-back, meaning 28 services in the days when church meetings could, and often did, last three or four hours each. It was grueling for them both but they were in it together, come what might. And, they never faltered in their belief that God would sustain them and see them through come what might.

"I wouldn't take nothin' for the life I've had," she would say often and did say the afternoon before her sudden home-going. "I loved bein' a preacher's wife." In true Mama fashion – she was never above bragging on herself – she would add, "And there ain't never been a preacher who had a better wife than Ralph Satterfield did."

I would agree.

As eternity, framed by an enormous hunter's full moon, loomed near for Daddy and his breaths were running out, his loved ones gathered in my childhood home waiting for his appointed time to meet the Lord. From my place on the sofa in the den, I saw Mama come to the door of the bedroom. She motioned me toward her.

Calmly and softly, she whispered, "I think he's gone."

In the marriage bed, the one she had bought with the money she saved from her 18 cents-an-hour hosiery mill job when first they wed, he had taken his last earthly breath as she sat beside him and gently stroked his face. A mighty warrior had faced his last earthly hurtle with his ever faithful gladiator by his side.

For Mama, though, the best was yet to come. With Daddy off to his heavenly reward and settled, no doubt, into comfortable everlasting eternity, life was all about her.

And she loved every minute of it. She was the center of everyone's attention – at least those who were smart enough to know the right way to act – and she was no longer a supporting character. As the good Lord would have it, and, in truth, it was probably her reward for a life of dedicated service, Daddy's home-going coincided with my newfound career as an author, a speaker and, a bit later, a columnist. Whenever the opportunity arose, which was often, she tagged along for my engagements and appearances. Mama basked in the reflected glory and would often tell people at book signings, "I always knowed she would make somethin' of herself. I just wish her daddy had lived to see it." Mama was excellent at giving a compliment that could double as a put-down.

As Mama liked to say, "The Lord can make something good out of anything bad." And that's what happened. Mama had lost the steadfast love of her heart after 58 years of serving as his ever faithful right hand. Her entire life and much of her identity had been wrapped up in family and service to God. It is during the moments of grief that a woman, who is up in years, can crumble, take to her bed and start counting off how many days she may have left to endure. Not Mama. The timing of my new book career and all the excitement and media it brought, energized Mama to the point that she looked a good ten years younger. After three years of nursing and seeing after Daddy in his decline, her laughter returned with a joyous ring, the exact sound which had never been heard by any of us. Our hearts were breaking over losing the rock that kept us steady and solid, yet seeing Mama emerge from her grief and find a new purpose and happiness helped our sorrowed hearts to ease. After six decades of a life that was always in service to someone else – a husband, children and grandchildren – she was unencumbered completely. "This is my time," she said when a year of mourning had passed. "It's all about me." She clasped her hands together and giggled. "I'm really lookin' forward to this. I'm gonna get out and enjoy loafin'."

Mama, the woman who loved the life she created when she courageously left the poverty of the mountains, had always felt happy and blessed. For the last years of her life, she often felt she was living in a dream. After a book signing in Oxford, Mississippi, I was gathering my things to leave and went to find Mama. She was sitting at a little table with a woman standing by her. Mama had pen in hand and was signing something.

"What are you doing?" I asked.

"I'm signing my autograph on your book."

"Why?"

She straightened up, pulled her shoulders back, smiled beatifically and pointed to the lady. "Because she asked me to." She was very proud.

I smiled and folded my arms across my chest. "It's my book. I wrote it."

She nodded. "Yeah but I made you so it started with me." She threw back her head and laughed happily. "I'm a celebrity." Charmingly, she tossed that crooked forefinger my way. "Get used to it."

That's right. She made me. She also made me mad, made me ugly when she cut my bangs crooked far too many times in my childhood years, made me remember to pray and trust in God, made me pretty when she sewed me a new frock, made me a great biscuit maker, made me smart she claimed by going to bed during her pregnancy with me and reading the encyclopedia through to the letter N before going into labor. "Who knows what all you would have done if I had made it all the way through 'Z'," she said.

The last ten years, though, she made me happier than I would have been without her steadfast, entertaining company plus she gave me memories that are among the cherished of my life.

Mama The Celebrity. Who would ever have thought?

Mama, Scotch-Irish thrifty always, made this apron and wore
it for 50 years despite the torn pocket and stubborn stains.

My readers meet Mama

She was there practically from day one. My newspaper readers met Mama in the third column in which I wrote about a car trip that included the mother of a friend of mine. I had invited her to join Mama and me because she had been feeling lonely. Sometimes Mama astounded me with what seemed like a cock-eyed view of things. She could definitely be self-centered and completely righteous about it when she was. I don't think I ever saw her scoot down a church pew in order to courteously allow someone to sit down. She took her seat on the end of the pew and stuck to it like glue. If someone else wanted to sit on our pew, she moved her knees to the side so the person could climb over her. It could be terribly embarrassing.

"If I had been your mama," I told her one Sunday after church when she had pulled that little stunt twice, "I would have raised you better."

"Well, I *was* your mama and I wish *I* had raised *you* better," she shot back. It was hard to one-up Mama.

The Baptists and Their Seats

Mama and I were planning a day trip. Nothing special, just a drive through the mountains, lunch at a charming restaurant and a little light shopping. I phoned the matriarch of the family the day before to tell her that a friend would be joining us.

"Fine," Mama replied. "She can sit in the back seat."

Mama wasn't being ungracious or inhospitable. She was simply being a good Baptist. See, with Baptists, it's all about where you sit. Seating in the Baptist churches ranks right up there with baptism by full submergence. Ask any regular church-going Baptist where she sits and down to the nail in the pew, she will tell you. "I sit on the left side next to the third window. There's a pulled thread in the carpet right there."

Ask any Methodist and the answer will be general such as "Well, we like to sit on the left side. But sometimes we sit on the right side. Just depends."

The Presbyterians will say, "Anywhere there's a seat." The Episcopalians, though, are seated according to giving. That's what I think, anyway, because I notice that the richer they are, the closer they sit toward the front.

I also know a suspiciously large number of Episcopalians who used to be Baptists. They were Baptists when they were poor but when they got rich, they switched. Just for the record, John D. Rockefeller was a tithe-giving, fully committed Baptist until the day he died. Not that it matters. It could have been that he just wanted to stay a Baptist where he could continue making up his prayers as he went and didn't have to go to the trouble of memorizing a whole book full of them.

But I bet he had his special seat at the Baptist church. And I bet that no one dared to sit there, either. Baptists are very territorial about their seats.

I go to a fairly large Baptist church, not like the little country church in which I grew up. Besides the significant difference in attendance, we now have a baptismal pool *inside* the church. I, on the other hand, was baptized in a cold river. We also had a cemetery where people could be buried for free.

In the little church, we read from the King James Bible, sang "I'll Fly Away" and gatherings that included food were always covered dish socials, not catered events. There are other differences, too. The preacher is paid better at the big church. He doesn't subsist solely on love offerings and bushels of vegetables from summer gardens or hogs that are grown fat, expressly with the preacher's family in mind. But one thing hasn't changed. People in big Baptist churches command control of their seats just the same as the ones in little country churches.

"Where do you sit?" someone in the choir recently asked.

"On the right hand side, 12th pew back, near a large column, on the end, next to the inside aisle."

"Who sits near you?"

"The Pooles are to my left and the Cabes to my right."

"Ah," he replied with a smile. "I know exactly where that is."

Once I visited my sister's church and she moved me four times before she found a seat that didn't "belong" to someone else.

As for my friend who drove to the mountains with us,

she didn't mind at all sitting in the back seat. She goes to my church, too, so I know for a fact that she sits on the back pew on the right-hand side every Sunday.

Being the committed Baptist seat keeper that she is, she felt right at home.

———— • ————

I didn't write about Mama until twelve columns later. Since my column runs weekly, that means it was almost three months before readers heard another Mama story. But when I told this one, women sympathized because every daughter has been put down or put in her place by her mama. The response for this one was so quick and enormous that it was my first inkling, as Mama liked to say, of what a popular character she would be.

One year after Daddy died, my first book, *What Southern Women Know (That Every Woman Should)* was published. My New York publisher put me on a national tour to promote it and, lo and behold, after an appearance on *The View*, the book hit best-seller lists. BellSouth (now owned by AT&T) then sponsored an additional week-long tour across Mississippi at some of the South's most noted bookstores that included Lemuria in Jackson, Reed's Gum Tree in Tupelo, Brown's Book Mart in Starkville, Square Books in Oxford, one in Natchez, Bookends in Bay St. Louis (Katrina would blithely swipe away this lovely place, both the town and bookstore) before ending the trip with a wonderful day spent in Fairhope at Page and Palette. This was back in the days (1998) when independent booksellers could and did make many a bestseller. My book was one of those. These wonderful independent folks would find a book they loved and hand-sell it to customers looking for a recommendation. My book rose to the Top 5 on the independent booksellers' lists and stayed in various other positions for a few months.

I invited Mama to hit the road with me and she was delighted to accept. It turned out to be one of the happiest weeks of either of our lives, though it didn't start out that way. Mama used to say, "Bad beginning, good ending." That proved true and accurate for the trip that Mama and I took to Mississippi. Along the journey, memories accumulated. Mama had stayed in a motel room only two or three times in her life and those had been 30 or more years earlier. We took my rescue dachshund, "Highway" (named because I had rescued her from the roadside), with us so I had to pay a pet deposit at the Holiday Inn in Jackson. We were there for two days. When I returned from a morning radio interview and a noon television show, Mama was all packed and ready to move on to Oxford.

"Looky," she said, smiling broadly, as she motioned around the little suite we had. "I cleaned and scrubbed it good so you'll get your deposit back." It was $25 and it had been promised to be returned if Highway did no damage. Motel management did not mean that we had to make the beds and clean the room. But Mama did. She had scrubbed the bathroom, dusted, made the beds and picked up lint off the floor. And, oh how proud she was. I started laughing.

"Mama, you didn't have to clean the room! They have housekeepers who do that. I'll get the money back because she didn't chew anything up."

She lifted her head. "There ain't one person who could clean this room better than this. Mark my words. Just tell the housekeepers not to bother to come."

I got the deposit back and delighted the front desk folks with the story of Mama cleaning the room.

"That's a first," the manager said, laughing.

"And, the last, I'm sure," I replied. "Mark this day down."

She signed books in Oxford after entertaining the people who came to see me with her stories. It was growing late and we needed to get on the road to Tupelo where we were to spend the night since I was doing television the next morning before my lunch time book signing. Mama was entertaining several women with the story of her courtship with Daddy.

"Mama, we need to go," I urged.

"But they want to hear *my* stories," she protested. "Don't you?"

"Your mama is really something," one woman said while Mama beamed from ear-to-ear and her eyes danced with joy. You could never brag on Mama too much. Sometimes when we were out and Mama thought I interrupted someone voicing a high opinion of her, she would say,

"Now, hush, Ronda. She's braggin' on me. Don't interrupt her."

Another woman chimed in, "She should write a book. I'd buy it."

Mama was on a high as we drove to Tupelo. "I've had the best time. Those people just loved me."

When we got to the Holiday Inn, she asked, "What are we going to do about Highway?" In those days, few motels accepted dogs. If I asked and they didn't, we'd have to go looking for another motel. It was already after 11 p.m.

I thought for a second and replied decisively, "We're going to follow President Clinton's lead with the military.

Don't ask. Don't tell."

She laughed. "Okay. I'll help you sneak her in." She was a cheerful co-conspirator. The next morning we were gone from the room by 7 a.m. so I could appear on a local television show. Our mission to hide Highway had been successful and we partners in crime were bonded together stronger.

At every restaurant where we stopped along the way, Mama would focus carefully on the menu. Each time, we would repeatedly send away the waitress while Mama studied the menu as though it was an obituary that she was memorizing. Finally, I would say, "Mama, just order chicken." It was the only thing she ever ordered that she did not complain about.

"I don't want chicken." She'd pooch out her lower lip. "Yes, you do. Just get that."

"It would be nice if you were a little more helpful to me." She lowered the menu and looked at me.

"Mama, I am being nice. Chicken is the only thing you ever order that you don't complain about. I'm being nice by helping you to get to the right solution quicker. I'm a big help."

Eventually, she would order chicken, always breaded and fried.

The night we drove Highway 90 into Gulfport, following it along the coast as a big full moon spotlighted the sea, Mama caught her breath. "Oh my goodness," she said, shaking her head. Few things impressed Mama but she was definitely in awe of what she saw. "There's the ocean. Ain't that something?" She had glimpsed the ocean only once when Daddy had worked in the shipyard in Newport News, Virginia before he joined the Navy to fight in World

War II. It was on this trip that she would marvel at the ocean on the Mississippi and Alabama Gulf coasts then in Florida, just over the Alabama line, when we stayed the night in a condo owned by Betty, the proprietor of Page and Palette.

"I just can't get over it," she said the next day. "All you can see is water. I wouldn't take nothin' for seein' this. It took me 78 years to get here but when you think about it, I've come a long way from bein' a little poor girl up in the mountains."

After a day in the storybook town of Fairhope, we drove six hours home, stopping in Opelika, Alabama, to get gas and pick up a copy of the Sunday edition of the *Atlanta Journal Constitution* that featured a complimentary review of my book.

"Oh, Ronda," Mama said when she finished reading the review. "I'm so proud."

It was after midnight when I pulled the car into her drive, one week and 15 hours after we had begun the journey that would include Mama telling her stories while my recorder taped as we drove along the Natchez Trace. While I was unloading the car, Mama stopped me. The moon was still big, waning slightly from its fullness in Gulfport a couple of nights earlier.

"I've had the best time," she said, smiling sweetly. She did possess one of the sweetest smiles possible when she chose to use it. She had great discretion, though, as to when she would charm and disarm with that smile. "You don't know how much this has meant to me. I've been so lonely since Ralph died but this trip has really boosted my spirits. It's just what the doctor ordered." She paused. "I'm really gonna miss you. It's gonna be even lonelier now after this week."

My heart melted. I hugged her. "I'm so glad you went. I love you."

"I love you, too."

It was such a special moment. A few minutes later, she stood on the porch in the same spot where she had been standing when I pulled in a week earlier. This time she stood in the light of the porch. I opened the door on the driver's side and looked at her. Her eyes filled with tears then mine did, too.

"I hate to see this end," she said. "I hate so bad to see you go."

"Me, too." I smiled, pushing the lump down in my throat. "We'll do other trips."

She nodded. "I hope so."

"I promise. Bye, Mama." I climbed in the car and wiped a tear from my eye. The trip sure ended a lot differently than it started. But that's often the story of such mother-daughter sagas. The column that follows became a story that I have told often in speaking engagements. Without question, it is one of my most popular.

Mamas

Why is it that your mother will say the worse thing possible to you, worse than your biggest enemy will even dare to think? Mothers will say it and never think twice about the hurt, havoc or humiliation it delivers.

They say whatever they want and then move easily, without a moment's hesitation, onto the next thought in their minds, which will have nothing to do with the harsh insult they just dropped into your lap. My mama will lift one eyebrow, cast a head-to-toes glance filled with disapproval and say sternly, "That skirt's too short. I'm not going out with you, showin' your tail like that. It's disgraceful."

My anger will quickly rise but I'll bite it back and say tersely, although I try to sound nonchalant, "Then don't go. Stay home."

"I am not stayin' home!" she'll shrill. "I spent an hour getting ready and you know what a hard time I have tryin' to fix my hair with my bad hand. I just can't hardly maneuver the curling iron since I had that little stroke years ago. After all that trouble, I'm not about to stay home."

That's mama. You can't go with her and you can't go without her. "Well, I'm not changing clothes so it would appear that you have a decision to make."

Know this – no car ever leaves mama's driveway without her well-covered tail planted firmly inside. For that reason, I'm always certain that I have the upper hand. She'll simmer for a moment and then say, "I'll go but you can bet on me tellin' people that *I* didn't raise you to be a floozie. You learned that all on your own."

I am not the only one with this problem. Sometimes

when my girlfriends get together, it is a subject of great conversation – our mamas and their comments. It's hard, though, for any of them to top my entertaining mama. She called me one night after watching a television show about Southern women that I had hosted. "You looked great," she began. "But the more I watched it, the more I realized that the reason you looked so good was because those other women looked so bad that they made you look good."

Once I made the questionable decision of taking mama with me on a seven-city book tour through Mississippi. That isn't just another story, that's another book. One that will not be published until Mama has gone to her heavenly reward.

No sooner had we settled into our seats and were fastening our seat belts than Mama looked over at me and began to lament over how bad I looked. She surmised that all of my travel and work had taken its toll on my appearance and was ravaging my looks. I shrugged. "I'm okay. It's just the shade of my lipstick. It's paler than I normally wear."

She clucked her tongue and shook her head sadly. "No, it's not. I can't believe how bad you look." She looked out the window and sighed. "And, it's such a shame because you used to be such a pretty girl." Wisely, I decided we would not get in a fight before we left the driveway so I held my tongue. She reached over to pat my dachshund, Highway, who was traveling with us and then chuckled. "Your brother said that the only reason I'm getting to go to Mississippi is to be the dog's nanny."

"Well, he's wrong."

Her smile broadened. "Really?" she asked, thinking I was about to brag on her.

"I'm taking you so that *if* I start to feel too good about myself, you can just bust my bubble."

Mama grinned happily. She loves having an important role in my life.

— · —

When I realized how women connected with stories of Mama by the amount of mail that came in, I followed up with a story three weeks later. This, too, involved a trip that started out on the wrong foot but, as went so many of our episodes, ended up well.

We both got so mad at each other that, as soon as we met up on the road with my cousins, Mama climbed out of my car and insisted that my cousin, Susan, ride with me so Mama wouldn't have to. When we arrived in the Smoky Mountains, Mama said, "I had a much better time ridin' with Dinah. She doesn't treat me ugly and she's so excited that I made chicken and dumplings." She lifted her chin in defiance.

That was another part of the rub. Not only had Mama gone against the agreement that had been made – we'd eat our meals out, which I was looking forward to because I ate at home except when I was traveling – she had made something she knew I didn't eat: chicken and dumplings. I don't eat chicken going back to childhood when I watched Mama, woman of the mountains that she was, grab a chicken out of the pen, wring its neck and prepare it for cooking.

In a day or two, we were over our mad spell, as was normally the case; but when I wrote about it, daughters across the South harmonized and connected because most daughters understand, at some point, how it feels to have an unruly mama.

Of course, that was not our last trip. Fortunately, there were many more to come which made great memories for us both as well as a couple of arguments connected with them (there was one in Natchez in the middle of a historic graveyard which is particularly memorable). The last 10 years of her life, Mama traveled many times more than she had traveled in her entire life. For both of us, it was worth the occasional aggravation of a fuss. The following column sprung up from that trip to Pigeon Forge.

The Last Trip (Which It Really Wasn't)

It appears that Mama and I have taken our last road trip together. This has become necessary because that woman simply won't mind me. Let me explain.

Somewhere along the road of life, we two Southern women have unwittingly exchanged roles. It is now she who is the stubborn, unruly child who does just as she dog-gone pleases despite my best psychological maneuvers which begin with reasoning, move to "laying down the law," onto logical discussions that progress to no nonsense demands, the firm putting-down-of-foot before ending with arguments that are not pretty. After our most recent trip – a two-day foray to my cousin Dinah's mountain re-treat – I have dispatched her figuratively to her room for somber reflection.

Perhaps she will come around to my way of thinking. But I doubt it.

Our main conflict revolves around Mama's packing. Without fail, I arrive to pick her up to find that she has dragged several bags out onto the front porch in eager anticipation of the forthcoming adventure. My jaw clinches the moment I pull into the driveway and see the scattered display. I can travel for a week with a small Pullman that fits easily in the overhead compartment of a plane. Same when I drive. One bag. That's it. Mama, on the other hand, travels heavy. This, of course, is no problem for her since she only carries her purse. Guess who totes all the other six bags she takes? Wisely, I decided to end the conflict by buying her a small suitcase like mine.

"It has wheels so you can handle it easily," I explained before adding sternly, "From now on, when you go with me, you take that suitcase. And only that one. If you don't, you're not going with me *anymore*." I thought that would put the almighty fear in her since she hates to miss out on a road adventure.

It worked as well as some of the ultimatums she used on me during my youth.

That was several trips ago and she has yet to take the tags off the suitcase I bought. She persists in using a collection of smaller bags, enough that it always takes me three trips to the car to load them. I am relieved, though, that she doesn't use brown Winn-Dixie bags to haul around her nightgown like my grandmother did. She called it a "paper poke." To add injury to misery on this last trip, she cooked a few pots of food *after* we had all agreed that we would dine out while gone. To add salt to the injury, she cooked things that she knows I don't eat.

"This is your last trip with me," I said, fuming.

She poked out her lower lip. "I'd be ashamed if I was you. What will you say if something happens to me and this really was my last trip?" Mamas revel in using this tactic.

"I'll say that I'm a prophet."

I know that bringing food to your host is a Southern woman's perfect sign of graciousness. But the point is that my mama doesn't listen to me. She's acting just like I did when I was 16. It's terrible and somehow I must gain control.

Does anyone know at what age your mama starts to mind?

I think, though, that I am finally beginning to understand. My mama used to promise repeatedly and emphatically that one day I'd pay for my raising when I had children of my own. So, I decided to outsmart both her and fate by not having children.

But I'm the one who got outsmarted because I am, indeed, paying for my raising. Mama, always determined to be right, is seeing to that.

———— • ————

When I found this next column while working on this book and read it, I tried my best to remember exactly what book it was that had gone missing and caused this fight. Though I'm blessed with an incredibly sharp memory, this one escaped me. Which goes to show that many things we argue about are keenly unimportant on down the road. When, years later, I found the book on my bookshelf, my heart sank because I couldn't apologize to Mama for my grievous mistake. I could only ask forgiveness from the good Lord. I recall that the argument started on the way to church which is when many of our disagreements started.

"That's the devil for you," Mama was oft to say.

When we slid into the pew that morning, I had my cousin sit between us because, as I explained, "We're mad.

She lost something of mine." Mama puffed up mad and said, "I didn't lose it. She blames everything on me and I'm getting tired of it." My cousin laughed. By the time church was over, the good Lord had done His work so we went out to lunch together and "acted like we had some sense" as Daddy used to say. At this point, it has been well over 12 years ago so either it was found or it didn't matter that much. If it was found, I apologize, albeit too late, to Mama. For the rest of y'all, let it serve as a lesson that sometimes fusses aren't worth the effort.

A Sunday Morning Fight

"I hope," Mama said the other day, "that I live long enough to see you write something nice about me."

A smile tugging at the corners of my mouth, I replied, "I hope I live long enough to find something nice to write." I stopped and grinned. "Hey, I have an idea. Why don't you work on giving me some *nice* material?"

For the record, less you think otherwise, my mama is a good, hard-working, God-fearing, decent woman who would do anything for any member of her family, especially me, her baby. She can, though, be mighty aggravating on more than an occasional basis.

She paused to think about what I had said then nodded and flung an agreeing finger in my direction. "I'll work on that."

I didn't get my hopes up. And it's a good thing, too, because a short time later we were both mad and pouting about the disappearance of one of my favorite childhood books. I got it when I was 11, and since it's now out of print, it sells for a lot of money. I decided to get it out of the desk in my old room and take it home with me. When I opened the drawers of the little antique desk, I found nothing that belonged to me because all of my childhood treasures had been replaced by Mama's things.

Unfortunately, this happened when I stopped by to fetch her for church one Sunday morning. After the argument that erupted, it is fair to say that by the time we arrived for church, neither of us were in a Christian frame of mind but the devil was very happy to have us representing him in the midst of the righteous.

A friend later commiserated, "If I had all the comic books and baseball cards that my mama has thrown out, I could put my children through college."

That didn't help my feelings.

I began to wonder how history survives memorabilia-tossing, treasure-throwing-out mamas like mine. In the library archives at the University of Georgia is a childhood treasure to behold. It is the first story ever written by a future Pulitzer-Prize winning author by the name of Margaret Mitchell. At the age of 11, she wrote an astounding story of a young girl named Margaret who traveled to the West and met cowboys and Indians. Mary Ellen Brooks, who oversees the archives, allowed me to hold that tiny book in my hands and marvel at the brilliance of Mitchell's story-telling prowess at such a young age. She hand-printed the text then bound it together in a little book. It is astounding.

But how would we know it was astounding if Margaret Mitchell had had a history-disregarding mother like mine?

Despite Mama's best efforts to eliminate my childhood things, I do have the first story I ever wrote. That, however, is owed to the competence of my second-grade teacher, Mrs. Elizabeth Rudeseal, who packed it away and saved it until a few years ago when she sent it directly to me, bypassing my mother.

"One day, I'll find that book you're looking for," Mama vowed. "And when I do, you'll owe me an apology."

Again, I'm not getting my hopes up or my apology prepared.

But I can't stop thinking about Margaret Mitchell and that precious treasure at the UGA Library. All I know is we can all be grateful that she didn't have a mother like mine.

If she had, that first little book of hers would be long gone with the wind.

———— • ————

This one has become a much-beloved story in the Mama legacy. Though we were headed – again – to church when this one popped up, I swallowed a reply and let it go. Not long ago, the preacher who was the pastor of that little church – one that Daddy had served – came up to me at a church homecoming and said, "Do you remember me and that day you played the piano at my church?"

I laughed, shaking his hand while I placed my other hand on his shoulder and replied, "Yes, I most certainly do. And do you remember how bad I was?"

He threw back his head and laughed merrily while nodding in the affirmative. "You meant well."

In engagements, I generally will tell this one during a church event and, almost always, will end the show with it because people like to leave with the taste of laughter in their mouths. It is also included in *What Southern Women Know About Faith*.

The Piano Player

As Mama was settling into the car and snapping her seat belt, I said – because I have no more sense than to open up a can of worms – "I changed clothes three times this morning before I settled on wearing this."

She threw a sideward glance toward me and the black dress encrusted with turquoise-colored beads and commented disapprovingly, "And then got one that barely covers your tail." She shook her head.

I bit the inside of my lip. I am trying hard these days not to get in a fight with Mama on the way *to* church. My goal is to wait until *after* church. It is, I believe, the Christian thing to do.

We had decided to visit a little country church in the mountains that is tucked between massive rolling hills amidst large oak and maple trees that hover majestically in protection over the sweet white-painted, cinder block church. Nearby, clear river water rolls toward small towns and large cities. It is in that river where the little church, Union Baptist, baptizes the newly converted.

We arrived for church moments before it started and greeted those we hadn't seen in the previous two years since the last time we attended service at that church.

"Do you play the piano?" asked Tony, one of the deacons.

"I used to," I replied, without thinking how unusual the question was. It had been many years since I touched the keys of a piano.

"Hey!" he called toward the choir loft. "Ronda can play the piano."

My eyes flew wide and my mouth dropped. I spun my head around in shock and, speechless, gawked at him.

"We ain't got no piano player today and we prayed that the Lord would send us one." He smiled broadly. "And He sent us you."

"Well, he didn't send much. I can tell you that," I replied.

And that's how I came to play the piano for the first time in 15 or 20 years for a church service. They had to sing what I could play, which wasn't much but we did find six songs. To say I was awful would be kind. But we managed.

"When you ain't got nothin'," a little lady said after the service, "anything will do."

Driving home, Mama and I, in a head-shaking, eyebrow-scratching kind of way, talked about the experience.

"Daddy used to say, 'Humble yourself before God.' I don't think I've ever been more humbled," I commented.

"What really amazed me," Mama replied in earnest candor, "was how you weren't a bit embarrassed by how bad you was."

Behind my sunglasses, I rolled my eyes. After all, a little encouragement or praise for my brazenness in displaying my serious lack of talent would have been nice. And, I might add, most welcomed. I ignored the comment.

"You know what I kept thinking while I was playing?" I asked with a light chuckle. "How much daddy must be laughing up in heaven."

"You know what I kept thinking?" she asked.

And, again, because I hadn't learned better, I asked, "What?"

"That I couldn't believe that you were sitting on a piano

bench in the middle of church in a dress that barely covered your tail."

Lord, have mercy on me.

I think that through my recent humility, I have, at least, earned that.

A jar of green beans from Mama's last canning and the battered tin cup she always used when canning tomato juice.

It just gets better

Mama drew people to her. It was astounding to watch. If Mama was in a good mood, she brightened herself up, turned the charm and storytelling on full tilt and she became the star of any room she entered. If she wasn't in a good mood, she broadcast that equally well. Many are the times that I found her sitting in a chair surrounded by several people completely enthralled as she expertly wove her stories. Mama also grew prettier as she aged and always looked much younger than she was. It was common that I would go looking for her so we could leave wherever we were and she'd say to one of her followers, "Tell Ronda what you said." She giggled and grinned ear-to-ear.

"I can't believe she's 80! I just don't believe it."

Mama was having heart problems after years of lard and Crisco. She was in the hospital to have tests and was eating at 4 p.m., the first food she had had since the previous day. I was sitting by the bed as she ate. The heart surgeon with chart in hand walked in and looked up. When he saw her, he looked back at her chart then stuck his head out the door to look at the name on the room.

"Are you Mrs. Satterfield?" he asked in a puzzled tone.

Mama didn't stop eating to answer. She just nodded and put another piece of biscuit in her mouth.

"How old are you?"

"I'll be 85 in June."

He looked at me. "Is that correct?"

"Yes, it is."

He started asking questions and when she didn't have food in her mouth, she answered. Finally, he said, "I came in here to tell you that I don't do heart surgery on patients as old as you but you look and act 70, so I'm going to do the surgery. You are amazing. A very handsome woman."

Mama, who had sworn up and down that she'd just go see Jesus sooner rather than have open-heart surgery, smiled from ear to ear. "That'll be fine. When do you want to do it?"

"Well, doctor," I replied wryly, "you said the right things: You told her that she's young and pretty so she's changed her mind about surgery."

Mama was predictably unpredictable and ridiculously 'set in her ways' as we say in the mountains but she was always interesting.

Knowing Better and Doing Better Are Two Different Things

I know better than to criticize myself when my mother is around. She always agrees.

"My hair looks awful," I said more to myself than to her as we passed a department store mirror and I stopped to take a look.

She nodded, "I know."

She ignored the look I threw her, which was, in reality, uglier than my hair. "I was just thinking a little while ago that you looked like a little orphan girl." She paused for a second and frowned. "That's not really fair to say." I couldn't believe my ears. She was going to retract a criticism. Then, she continued. "Little Orphan Annie never looked bad like that. I use to read her in the funny pages."

I have learned not to retort with her. My words are too sharp and, besides, I can't win. So, I said nothing. I just tried to smooth down the disheveled mess.

But she can't stop. She'll always offer analysis.

"I think you're ruining your hair with all the stuff you put on it. It's probably just dry and brittle."

I decided to retort. "My hair is in perfect condition. It is not dry and brittle."

"Did you use hairspray?"

"Yes."

"Because it don't look like you used hairspray. If you sprayed it real good, it wouldn't look like that. Are you sure you used hairspray?"

"Yes, I'm sure."

"Well, what kind did you use?"

"An expensive kind."

"Then you should change brands. It doesn't look like to me that the one you're using is worth a dime."

I resisted the urge to retort further. I decided to wait and even the score. I knew my time would come. I was smug about it. Just as an aside: This is how many wars are lost – people get arrogant before victory. My time to even the score took its time coming but it finally showed up a couple of weeks later when we arrived together for a family get together. Mama worries about her looks more than I do, especially when she's going to be anywhere near some-one who might brag on her. She was walking a few steps ahead of me when, suddenly, she stopped and turned to ask, "Do I look okay?" She stood up straighter than normal, smoothed her skirt and smiled prettily as if the smile would make the outfit better. Before I could answer, she continued. "I shouldn't have worn this. I'll probably have on the worse lookin' outfit here."

My chance had arrived. I nodded, being sure that I gave her a serious once-over like she would give me. "Why on earth did you wear that anyway? You have much prettier clothes."

That did it.

Mama, though, doesn't handle me as well as I handle her. I ignore her but she takes my words seriously.

"I'm going home." She turned back toward the car. "I'm not going in, looking like something the cat drug in."

Of course that's not what I had in mind. I only wanted to aggravate her but it ended up being an aggravation to me. Because I then had to spend the next several minutes coddling and reassuring her that she looked beautiful and that I was only teasing. Finally, grudgingly, she went in. I sneaked around and whispered to a few, begging them to brag on her outfit. They did but also others, who didn't know I needed help, complimented her. Mama is truly a handsome woman and always, to her delight, chalks up many words of praise. Once a few people had commented kindly on her outfit, she relaxed.

But, as usual, she got in the last word.

"We need to come back another time and see all these people," she announced as we were driving away. I assumed it was because of all the attention she had received.

"Why?"

"Because I'd like 'em to see you sometime when your

hair doesn't look so bad." She took a long, appraising look. "Otherwise, they're gonna think you look like this all the time."

Does anybody know where I can find a few good retorts?

———— • ————

This column still brings a lump to my throat. Mama was with me one night as I pulled the car up to my mailbox and wrestled out a huge load of mail. The wistful sound of her voice, as she surveyed the pile then shook her head sadly, still haunts me. This story would become the basis for a short speech I gave to a group of postmasters at their convention in Anchorage, Alaska. I told them of the difference they made in the lives of people like Mama and Miss Loretta when they delivered magic to them on ordinary days.

I ended the speech by saying, "So, on behalf of Mama and Miss Loretta and the others like them who have their days made special because of the mail you deliver, we thank you!" Four thousand postmasters leapt to their feet, clapping and cheering. They liked being reminded of the difference they make.

An old friend of mine, Miss Mary Jo, read the column, contacted me for Mama's address and, for the remaining few years of Mama's life, she sent her weekly letters and packages. Sometimes she would adorn them with glitter or cut-outs. She went to a lot of trouble but it made Mama so happy. One day, I walked in to find Mama sitting in her worn recliner with pen in hand and a piece of paper. "I'm writing Mary Jo to thank her for all the happiness she gives me."

Mama seldom wrote thank you notes, so on the rare occasion that she wrote one, she meant it. Sometimes she'd say, "I'm old. No one expects an old woman to write a note." A while later, when death had visited our family yet again, Mama wrote her friend on two pages of paper that she tore out from a composition book, to express her sorrow. Mary Jo kept the correspondences and returned them to me when Mama died. They are like spun gold to me though the letter of grief is painful to read. It is comforting, though, to see her cursive, sprawling handwriting. I have kept every scrap piece of paper that she wrote on even the "wash before cooking" notes stuck in the field peas she had shelled and frozen. In my safe deposit box are three letters she wrote when I was living in Indianapolis while working in NASCAR. I was utterly homesick but a letter from Mama in my mailbox was always pure joy. I am happy to say that this story struck a note with many folks, who then started sending cards and notes to elderly friends and family.

Send Cards and Letters

Mama said something the other day that just broke my heart.

Her words, so innocent and wistful, shot through my chest, grabbed my heart and twisted it into such a tangle that it still hasn't straightened out. It reminded me of how we of youth take for granted that which is valued so deeply by those of age.

She was in the car with me when I pulled up to my mailbox to retrieve the day's mail. As usual, there was so much of it that Melinda, my letter carrier, had bundled it together with three large rubber bands. It was a normal day's bounty, which is in addition to what I receive at my post office box. Enough that if I miss two days of working it, I'm hopelessly behind on personal correspondence, business matters, bills and catalog ordering; and my kitchen counter stacks up woefully. A few days out of town and Melinda greets my return with a huge box of mail so heavy that she can barely tote it to the front door.

And, without question, I am always despairing of the job required to tackle the massive mess.

But Mama made me rethink that.

I pulled the huge bundle from the mailbox and Mama said, with the kind of sigh a child would use in eyeing a new red wagon, "Oh, what I'd give to get an armload of mail like that."

What I'd give *not* to get that much on a daily basis, I thought immediately. Wide-eyed and disbelieving, I swung my head around and stared incredulously. "Are you serious?"

She nodded solemnly. "It's so lonesome to go to an empty mailbox. Sometimes I'm glad to just get a sales paper."

Gulp.

For those like my mama, widowed, aged and alone, a note or a card means more than two weeks in Hawaii would mean to my friends. It's something so simple but something that those of us who are blessed with busy lives take for granted.

I am ashamed.

I know better. That's even worse. I know how my friend, Miss Loretta in Cincinnati, eagerly watches the mailbox for a hand-written note from me. I try to write every couple of weeks. In her shaky 87-year-old hand-writing, she will write back of her glee when she goes to the mailbox and sees a note from me.

"I am always so excited to see you've written that I can't wait to get back to my apartment and read it. It's a treat, so I save it until my chores are done and I can sit down and enjoy it."

Miss Loretta keeps all my correspondence in a ribbon-tied bundle and re-reads them often. I know this because one day, unexpectedly, I showed up on her doorstep in Cincinnati and there were all my letters bundled and tied in ribbon beside her chair.

My sister, a postmaster, once told me about an elderly woman who met her carrier at the mailbox.

"Nothin' but junk mail today, Mrs. Jackson," the carrier said.

The woman smiled beatifically. "Oh honey, that's just fine. It's not junk when that's all you get. I'm just glad to get something."

Thanks to the wisdom that has finally begun to accumulate in my life, I realize that simple kindnesses are as important – sometimes more so – than the extravagant ones.

———— • ————

Mama loved gardening. When I was a kid growing up, we always had a vegetable garden with rows of tomatoes, green beans, peas, squash, okra and corn. Mama worked all summer to grow enough food to see us through the hot months then have enough to 'put up' for winter. I can still feel the wet, sticky corn all over me as we shucked and cut it and still I can smell the strong scent of tomato juice, which she would spend days making so that we'd have a winter filled with creamed tomato soup and hot cornbread.

When Daddy was sick and that took a lot of her time, Mama gave up the garden. After he died, my brother-in-law, Rodney, said, "Bonelle, how would you feel about me comin' down here with my tractor and plowing a few rows for you to have a little garden?"

A million dollars handed to her right then and there would not have made her any happier. She beamed. "I would love it!"

Since the old garden area had been fenced in to become part of the pasture, the only place that Rodney could plow was in the front of the house next to the road. He put in three long rows in which she planted mostly green beans and tomatoes, though she did have some peppers and squash. For the final summers of her life she took great pride in that little garden and how pretty it was.

When the green beans came in with terrific abundance, my niece, Nicole, and I were called into action to pick during the hottest summer that Georgia had ever known. Many days were well over 100 degrees. One night, Nicole and I were picking at 8 p.m. and it was still 97 degrees. It was miserable.

But Mama was happy.

Earlier that spring as the garden was still growing into a pretty sight, I went by to pick Mama up and take her to the grocery store. She got in the car and was clearly perplexed and bothered. As I backed out the driveway, she said, as she did every time we drove either in or out of the driveway, "Looky there, don't I have the prettiest garden you ever seen in all your born days?" Or something along those lines. Then she said, "I'll tell you – I'm really upset about somethin'."

"What?"

"I saw in the paper today where they're havin' garden tours. They're payin' people to let them come to their house and look at their gardens." The corners of her mouth turned down. "There ain't nobody got no prettier garden than me, so I want to know why I'm not on the tour?"

I started laughing so hard that I had to pull the car over and park so I could laugh. She looked at me quizzically.

"What's so funny?"

"Mama, they're not taking tours of vegetable gardens. They're lookin' at big flower gardens!"

She took the information, processed it for a moment then remarked, "Well, still, they oughta come here. Nobody can beat my green beans."

A couple of days later when we went out to eat, she reported that someone had been admiring her garden free of charge. "I was walkin' by the livin' room picture window when I looked out and seen a red pickup truck go by real slow. Then, it stopped, backed up and sat there for a while just lookin' at my garden. That truck should have paid me five dollars for that look."

I chuckled. "It was probably Rodney. Checking to see how good the garden he plowed was comin' along."

The next day when we saw Rodney, she said, "I wanna ask you somethin'. Did you come by in your red pickup the other day and look at my garden?"

He nodded. "Yep. Looks good. You're gonna have plenty of beans."

She held out her hand. "Pay up." She beamed.

I bent over double, laughing, while Rodney and my sister, Louise, looked completely buffaloed. Mama stood her ground. "There's people gittin' paid good money for other people to look at their gardens and ain't a prettier garden anywhere than mine. You looked at it for a mighty long time. You owe me five dollars."

Now, never mind the fact that Rodney had gone to all the trouble to load up his tractor and take it down to Mama's to plow and that she was just having fun. Rodney, as always, had a quick comeback.

"Bonelle, if you're gonna charge people to look at your garden, don't put it in the front yard next to the road where they can look at it for free."

Mama and The Green Beans

Yet, another queen has sprung up to reign in my family.

My mama has ascended to the royal throne to preside as Green Bean Queen. Over the summer, she earned this title by paying prodigious attention to her little garden, which consisted solely of green beans, tomatoes and a few cucumbers that weren't planted but popped up anyway. The poor tomatoes got little attention because the green beans got the royal share of love and nurturing.

Remember "Bubba" in the movie *Forrest Gump*? He was always thinking of ways to prepare shrimp?

That's mama with green beans. She can make green bean casseroles, green bean salads, green bean sandwiches (don't laugh until you've tried cold green beans on white bread with mayo spread generously), green bean soup, steamed green beans, green beans seasoned with ham, green beans fried with bacon grease, green bean bread, green beans boiled quickly then sauté with butter, and green beans tossed with grits.

And, she reasons, if you can make a pie from lemons and pudding from rice, why can't you make a cake with green beans? After all, a lot of sugar can hide a multitude of sins.

To be honest, it's just too many green beans for me. But it sure makes the Queen happy.

For three months, she lived solely for green beans. Before the heat of the day grew unbearable, she was in the garden attired in long sleeves, pants, my galoshes and her little red hat. Then, happily, she spent the rest of the day devoted to her green beans. She picked, strung, snapped and canned.

"Would you climb up there and check those cans of green beans?" she asked one day when I stopped by. "I want you to take the old cans down so I can throw them away."

On high shelves in the pantry, I found many cans of green beans that Mama had canned, dating back over 15 years to 1988 and all years in-between.

"Mama, this is ridiculous," I said as I pulled them down. "There are at least 10 cans of beans for every year back to 1988."

She looked at me imperially. "Why is that ridiculous?" Her Majesty asked.

I rolled my eyes. "Because it means that you don't need all the green beans that you can every year. Yet, you keep on growing them and canning them."

Her Royal Highness ignored me because her pressure canner was whistling her name.

One day, her obsession got to be too much. She needed flat lids but refused to buy them from the nearby small store that was charging $1.39 for a dozen lids.

"They're trying to put us small farmers out of business,"

she railed.

"A little green bean garden doesn't make you a farmer."

That was the comment that got me sent all the way into town to hunt down lids for $1.25. With the price of gas, I figure it cost me eight dollars to save Mama 28 cents for two dozen lids.

But she's the Green Bean Queen, so whatta you going to do?

As summer drew to a close, mama grew sad. "I don't know what in the world I'm gonna do without my green beans to take care of. It's gonna be awful lonely."

I felt sorry for her. "Well, maybe you could hold multiple titles. Some queens do."

"Like what?" she asked.

"I think you'd make a terrific Pumpkin Queen."

She smiled at the thought.

Does anyone know how fried pumpkin tastes?

—— · ——

Some of my stories come from the funeral home. In the South, whenever someone dies, we gather at the funeral home to pay respects and just visit with each other. Mama loved to go to the funeral home because people always made so much over her. One day, she called me and said, "I don't know what's wrong with me. I just feel so blue."

She talked on for a bit then I said, "You know what you need? A good trip to the funeral home. That always cheers you."

Her voice lifted. "You're right. That would do me a world of good. People always enjoy seein' me so much. It does them as much good as it does me."

Mama didn't drive so someone always had to take her to church, shopping or the funeral home. One day she called and needed to go to the funeral home. It was early evening and I was taking a long walk with my dog, Dixie Dew. I was a mess. No makeup, unwashed hair in a pony-tail and slumming-around-clothes.

"Mama, why didn't you call me earlier? It's time for visiting hours and I don't have time to dress, drive over to get you then drive another 25 minutes to the funeral home. I can't let people see me like this."

"Well, I can't help it. I fell asleep in my chair watchin' *Dr. Phil* so I was late gittin' to the mailbox to get my paper and read the obituaries. I didn't know he was dead. And, I still don't know what kilt him. I just got to go. We went to church with them for years. And you'll have to take me because Louise and them are gone sommers."

I sighed heavily. "Okay, I'll take you but I'm not going in. I'll sit in the car and wait on you."

This started all amounts of commotion because Mama didn't like to go in anywhere by herself. "I can't go in by myself," she said. "I have a complex."

"Oh, you don't have any complex. Stop it. That's the deal. Take it or leave it."

She took it but she wasn't happy. Trust me, though, she had plans to get even. We pulled into the parking lot, and after ten minutes of coaxing her and assuring her that she could, in fact, walk into the funeral home by herself, she got out of the car, slammed the door and stomped out. A few minutes after her skirt disappeared through the door, a group of five people I knew came out the door. It was night so I slid down in the seat so they wouldn't see disheveled me, but they walked straight to my car, tapped on the window and called, "Your mama said you were out here and we should come out and see you." I could have died from embarrassment.

I let down the window and began apologizing for how bad I looked. I was smoothing my hair and straightening my sweatshirt when three more people walked up. "Bonelle said you were out here and that you'd want to speak to us."

By the time Miss-Priss-With-A-Complex returned, about two dozen people had paraded out to talk to me. She got in the car and I was so mad that I couldn't see straight.

"I can't believe you," I said angrily. "You sent all those people out to see me when you knew I didn't want anyone to see me looking this way."

She smiled cheerfully and shrugged. "They were all asking how I got here so I told them that you brought me. And they wanted to see you, so I wasn't going to stop them."

Mama always won. No matter what. She won.

Since the following column has to do primarily with my sulking, I include it because it gives a glimpse into how truly cool and enjoyable Mama could be. She didn't try to talk me out of the sulking. Instead, she played along. It was moments like this that felt like we were actors in a situation comedy. And, of course, Mama had the starring role.

The Joy of Sulking

On the way home from a speaking engagement, my sister, Louise, called me on my cell phone.

"Whadda you doin'?" she asked as usual then quickly cut to the purpose of the call.

"Can you take Mama to the funeral home tonight?" she asked before explaining that the husband of a family friend had passed away.

Dadgum it. My heart sank. I had big plans for the evening. I was going home to sulk. After a battering day, I had promised myself the treat of locking myself away from the world and taking the entire evening to appropriately sulk.

Sulking is a woman's prerogative. It's very important to us that we get to indulge ourselves and do this every once in a while. A couple of times a year, I allow myself an evening of uninterrupted sulking. Then, the next morning I awake, and all the combative darkness has been freed from the soul; so I bounce back as good as new.

I really needed to be home sulking, not going to the funeral home, but I knew that Louise would never accept that as an excuse. So I sighed resignedly and mumbled half-heartedly, "Okay."

My dear friend Tim Richmond, a NASCAR superstar before his untimely death, used to badger me about my "pouting." Normally, this came after our routine bickering. I loved Tim, but anyone who knew him will tell you that it was mentally exhausting and emotionally depleting to be his friend. He was spoiled rotten and life was always all about him.

If I were unusually quiet, he would say, "Uh-oh. You're not pouting again, are you?"

"I'm not pouting, I'm moping. There's a difference."

"Really?" He'd cock his head to one side and look at me suspiciously.

"Pouting is when you're quiet because you're mad. Moping is when you're quiet because you're sad. You make me sad a lot, so I mope."

I have grown up now and matured from moping to sulking. It's very important, though, that sulking be done in the privacy of one's own home, away from everyone. The major rule of this female indulgence is that no one else should be exposed to it. That would be rude. And beholding to proper Southern womanhood, it is expected courtesy to stay away from people when you're not feeling bright and happy.

At the funeral home, Mama loitered at length, chatting happily away.

I tugged discretely at her sleeve. "Mama," I whispered. "Let's go home. I need to sulk."

She ignored me and sat down on the sofa for a long talk. Finally, I nudged her out the door and into the car. We had been there for over two hours.

"Let's stop and have dinner," Mama suggested. "I'll buy."

Mama offering to buy is so rare that I would never turn it down. Not even to sulk.

"Okay. But we have to make it quick. I've got to get home to sulk."

As soon as Mama laid her fork down, I grabbed up my purse and said, "Okay, let's go. We're wasting my sulking time."

When she got out of the car at her house, she looked back. "Hope you have a good sulk."

"Thanks," I replied. "I will."

And I did. Nothing beats a good sulk. I'm so glad that it's a prerogative of womanhood.

Mama's Star Get Brighter

When I wrote my first novel, based on a true experience that had happened to me while on a book tour, I included a mama character. Since the lead character was fairly auto-biographical so were the mama stories I told. I don't believe I made up one mama story for that book. There was no need to because Mama provided me with terrific material.

The Town That Came A-Courtin' brought tremendous joy to Mama. She, as well as other family members and friends, joined me to kick off the extensive book tour in Arkansas at That Bookstore In Blytheville, the wonderful town that had inspired the book. Mama patiently sat for television and newspaper interviews. She loved to tell any-one, who would listen, as to how I never dated in high school and did not go to any proms.

"She wasn't popular with the boys in high school," she would chatter as I seethed. "She was a wallflower. Of course, she was always a bit chubby and had freckles. Then, one day, lo and behold, she just blossomed out. She wasn't always pretty."

She signed autographs, rode in a limousine for the first time and posed for photos with her fans. The book became a best-seller which led to it being bought by *Reader's Digest* to be a condensed book as you will see in the story that fol-lows. Sometimes she would call and say, "I need a book to give to someone and it needs to be one with lots of stories about Mama because that's what people enjoy so much."

There's a part of me that wishes Mama had lived to see the movie that was made of that book and to see an actress playing her. Of course, as my sister, Louise, said when she watched it, "Mama would be beside herself that the woman playing Mama is showing her knees. I can hear her saying, 'I'll tell you one thing right now – I'd never be showing my tail like that.'"

Louise is right. That's why another part of me is glad she didn't live to see it. But, my oh my, how Mama would have loved being a movie star. The column that follows was written shortly after the book's publication.

Reader's Digest

Just when I thought that Mama's star had peaked and was beginning to fall, *Reader's Digest* called.

"Is your mother really like what you write or do you embellish it?" asked a Hollywood screenwriter.

I laughed. "No, she's not just like that. I tone her down a lot because if I wrote the precise truth, no one would believe it."

Green, the color of envy, slipped across his face. "You're lucky. I have to make up my characters and none of them are ever as colorful as Mama."

"If you don't stop writing about me, I'm gonna pinch your head off," Mama will say, pretending to complain. Then, if two weeks pass and she isn't mentioned in my column, she will call and say, "You need to write some more about Mama because it's not nearly as good or interesting without Mama in it."

This, of course, is simply the way it is with Mama – you can't win either way. Still, I've been trying to slip her gently into the background. She isn't going easily. First of all, she doesn't want to go. Second of all, readers refuse to let her go. For some reason, many find her captivating. She, apparently, is also a marketer's dream.

As in the case with *Reader's Digest*.

My New York editor called one day with unexpected, but happy news. "*Reader's Digest* has just paid a very nice advance for the rights to your novel," she announced. "They're going to reprint it in their Condensed Books series."

Now, any way you look at that, it's good news. It was especially sweet news to me because I grew up reading *Reader's Digest Condensed Books,* so I thought it was really neat that they wanted to do my book in the series.

Then the bombshell fell.

She cleared her throat before continuing. I am old enough and wise enough now to know that a throat is cleared just before something is said that is going to choke you. I had a boyfriend once who always cleared his throat just before he started lying. In other words, he was constantly clearing his throat.

I chewed my lower lip and waited.

"Someone over at *Reader's Digest* got on your website and found a picture of you and your mama. They want permission to use it in all their promotional materials."

I rolled my eyes and wondered if I was going to have to pay Mama. Then, I decided to take my chances against a lawsuit and answer on her behalf.

"That'll be fine," I replied. Actually, I think my chances for a lawsuit would have been higher if I had denied them the rights. Mama has grown fond of her fame. When we bickered over a column that she thought was too harsh, I declared emphatically that she was out of my column for good.

She didn't blink. She knew she had the upper hand and replied calmly, "If you do, you'll lose readers."

Once while eating out, a woman approached me in the restaurant and talked for several minutes of how much she enjoyed my column. Finally, Mama reached over and tugged at her sleeve.

"Hey," she said, grinning broadly. "I'm Mama."

The woman immediately dropped me like a hot potato and turned her attention to the real star.

"You'd better be careful," she warned with a wink when she found out that *Reader's Digest* was using her in their advertising. "I might get so popular that I shoot you out of the saddle."

That's a star for you. As soon as they make it big, they forget the little people who made 'em.

In this case, the little people would be me.

———— · ————

After Mama's triple bypass surgery, she was an absolute saint for a couple of weeks or so. Then, the goofy medicine wore off and she turned into a nightmare. Nothing suited her. One day, I brought her some potato soup that I had picked up at a new restaurant. She eyed it suspiciously then cautiously took a bite. She made an ugly face and said, "Here. Take this and find me somethin' fit to eat. I wouldn't feed that to the hogs."

Those few weeks of recovery turned into a Mother's Day column for me and, for the first time, landed me in seriously hot water with Mama. I had finally pushed it too far with her.

"I'm humiliated," she said then poked out her lower lip

and set her jaw. "I can't show my face because you've made me out to be a jackass. I don't know how I can ever hold my head up enough to go back to church."

Let's begin with the first column I wrote about her surgery. I love this one because it was typical Mama – she really cared how she looked and she believed in the power of lipstick. Following that is the Mother's Day column that caused the problem, then it is succeeded by the one where I put her on probation and took her out of the column. It nearly killed her and, as you will see, she kept on campaigning until she returned triumphantly to the pages.

"I helped make you what you are and if you stop writin' about me, you'll go down like the Titanic. Mark my words, little girl."

Pretty Mama

This is a true story. I swear on my favorite pair of Manolos (the hot pink stilettos) that it is.

Mama, despite a somewhat vigorous existence, had been feeling puny for a few months and, to be brutally honest, wasn't looking her best. It's probably a certainty that the suffering of her beauty not the suffering of her body was what got her, at long last, to go to Dr. Jeff Marshall, her beloved heart doctor.

Stories concerning my mother as well as those told by her are never short. This is not an exception. However, I will skip many details and tell you that Mama, downright contrary for months about having a heart catheterization, finally succumbed to it. Later, she was probably sorry because it led to a triple bypass surgery. Don't, though, mention anything to her about those years of staunch devotion to Crisco-frying catching up with her. She doesn't take it kindly.

True to form, she continued to be more concerned with beauty than with anything more serious.

Before she went for the test, she was absolutely convinced that she would end up having some procedure done so she began preparing. For days, she sorted, washed and mended, if necessary, her prettiest gowns. Mama has always had a strong affinity for beautiful gowns, so she has many.

"Look at this one," she said one day, holding up a pretty pink one with spaghetti straps. "I think I'll sew a wide piece of lace over the straps. It's just too naked for the hospital. Don't you think?"

She packed her bag, and my sister, Louise – her co-conspirator in all things pertaining to beauty – arrived to survey the bounty. Dutifully, the Queen Mother had packed her cosmetics, gowns and curling iron.

"You forgot your hairspray," Louise pointed out.

"No, I didn't." I knew that before she said it. Mama would never forget her hairspray. "I didn't pack it because I lost the cap to it and it's so expensive that I don't want to chance losing a drop of it."

"I don't care," Louise replied. "Pack it anyway."

Before she left her house for the heart catheterization, she prettied herself up appropriately. While she waited to be taken down for the procedure, she laid in bed while friends and family filed in to pay their respect and to comment on her loveliness.

"Why you look so pretty, it's hard to believe that you're not the picture of perfect health."

Mama smiled beatifically.

Then the nurse arrived to announce that they would be taking her down shortly. As soon as the nurse disappeared, Mama commanded, "Get my lipstick and let me put it on before I go."

Isn't it nice when a woman who has already spent eight decades on this earth still cares so much?

Mother's penchant for beauty, though, actually helped her. When the test revealed that she had three significant blockages, the surgeon, prior to seeing her, was hesitant because of her age. Then he saw the powdered-to-perfect maven and made his decision.

"Anyone who looks this young and vivacious needs to feel that way, too," he announced.

Mama smiled grandly. A little bragging goes a long way with her.

We continue to be grateful that our prayers were answered and Mama came through the surgery good while maintaining her perfect diva mentality.

The day after surgery, I visited her in ICU to tell her that others were waiting to see her.

"Do you feel like it?"

She nodded, eyes closed. "Okay."

I turned to leave when I heard her say softly, "Ronda?"

"Yes."

Eyes still closed, spirit sick and weak, she whispered, "How does my hair look?"

It's hard to keep a good diva down.

But then the problems begin....

Mother's Day, 2006

Mama, never one to hold back her opinion, was commenting on my latest columns.

"You know, they're just not as interesting when you don't write about me," she commented casually. "You haven't written much about me lately."

"That's because I haven't had anything nice to say and you always said that if you can't say anything nice about someone, don't say anything at all."

I wasn't kidding.

She cut her eyes over at me sharply. "Well, some of that stuff you write ain't that nice, if you ask me."

"Trust me. If I had been writing about you lately, it would be a lot worse."

She turned her nose up and signified that the matter was closed. No more discussion. But I've reconsidered. Since, after all, it is Mother's Day, I will give her the gift she most wants – a column all about her.

It's been tough the past few months since her triple bypass surgery. First of all, you have to be careful not to mention any dependency on Crisco oil or even remotely suggest that skim milk would be better for the ol' arteries than whole milk. In fact, more than one nurse or nutritionist has gone down over that last one.

During her surgery and the few weeks that followed, Mama was the model patient. She was sweet and appreciative for everything that my sister and I did for her. She even seemed to realize all the work time we were giving up for her. That's the kind of patient that you don't mind nursing.

Then one day, without warning, it all changed. Cranky

won't even begin to describe it. It was worse than a starving rattlesnake crawling through the heat-stricken desert.

She went from being funny mean to being just plain mean.

"What is wrong with you?" I asked her one day. "You're so mean lately."

"I know I am," she replied.

Now, that stopped me right there. Not only had Mama turned cranky, she had turned reasonable. Before the surgery, she would have disputed it and claimed that we were the aggravating ones, not her.

"You know you're mean?" I asked incredulously.

"I'm not myself since I had that surgery and looks like to me, y'all could take that into consideration."

"Consider it considered," I replied. "Now, could you please quit being so cranky?"

Mama might have turned reasonable with her surgery, but she hadn't turned cooperative. She continued to be cranky. So, during a checkup, I asked her doctor about it. In front of her. And I gave explicit examples. Like a child who knows she's been naughty, she listened quietly and contritely.

"It's normal," he said. "She's been through a tough ordeal so it'll take some time for everything to straighten out and her personality to return. This happens when someone has been on the bypass machine."

"Well, in the meantime, could you give her some pills for it?" I've come to learn that the medical field has pills for everything, so surely there's some kind of medication for orneriness.

He shook his head. "It just needs to wear its self out," replied the doctor whom I formerly loved. "She'll be fine in a few months. Wait and see."

A few months! I could have a nervous break-down by then. Then, I would be the one needing pills. Truth be told, I need them now.

The doctor was right, though. She's getting better and less cranky every day. Soon, I'll probably be back to writing about her. Meanwhile, Happy Mother's Day, Mama. Despite the crankiness, I'm glad you made it through your surgery so well.

Cranky or not, it just wouldn't be Mother's Day without you.

Then the solution…

Mama's Probation

In case you haven't noticed, Mama has been banished from this column for several weeks.

Have you missed her?

It all started when she, for the first time ever, took exception to a piece I wrote on her crankiness following heart surgery. If I thought she was cranky before the piece, it was nothing compared to what came after that one ran in the paper.

To make a long argument short, we exchanged quarrelsome words about it. To repeat what happened would not speak well for either of us. So, we'll keep that information locked in the big family vault of secrets.

But to my credit, before we had the argument, back when she was merely pouting about the cranky column, I did try to buy peace. I took her shopping and bought her a new outfit. I tried to smooth it over. She took the new clothes but in a few days was back to complaining. That's when it blew up.

I ended the argument by saying, "Okay, that's it. You're out of the column. I'm not writing about you anymore." Then, just as I have ended quarrels with Mama since I was six, I stormed out the door.

After many weeks, Mama is tired of being sidelined. She's ready to return to the starting lineup and rejoin Claudette, Debbie, Karen, Louise, Miss Virgie, Dixie Dew, Merri Grace and the other beloved ones that often appear in my stories.

She's quite a player, that mama of mine. The world powers have nothing on her when it comes to strategy.

"Ronda, people are very displeased that I'm not in your column," she said. "You wouldn't believe all the upset folks. Someone told me the other day that if you quit writing about me, you're gonna lose a lot of readers."

I rolled my eyes. I know when I'm being played. Still, once Mama starts, she doesn't stop until she's won. For two weeks, I received daily updates from her on all the folks who want her back in print. The cashier at the grocery store, the receptionist at the doctor's office, the beautician and the list goes on. She claims that the preacher is in prayer about it. Every day, the stories become more elaborate.

"This woman – I don't know her name, I just know her when I see her – she said, 'You're the best thing she writes about! We just love Mama stories.' She couldn't believe you weren't writing about me anymore." Mama shook her head in despair.

"You're making that up," I replied flatly.

"No, I ain't. It's the truth."

Then she decided to draw up a petition and pass it around for signatures, asking for her reinstatement.

"How many names do I need to win a reprieve?" she asked.

Enough already. I've decided to pull Mama off the sidelines and put her back in the column. On probation. So, we'll see how this goes.

"Okay, you're back. But only on probation," I warned. "If you get outta hand again, it'll be goodbye time."

She grinned jubilantly and clapped her hands together joyfully. "Oh, good! Everyone will be so happy."

Problem about that is that she's right. She and Dixie Dew, my dachshund, are overwhelmingly more popular than me.

But, honestly, it's not good for Mama to have so much popularity. What if she dies? Then what?

My brother-in-law cares for his mother who has battled Alzheimer's for many years. The other day, he was dressing her and she said, "Rodney, I love you so much. You're so good to me." She smiled sweetly. "I hope I die before you do."

Rodney chuckled good-naturedly. "Mama, that makes two of us."

I'm starting to think that just the opposite would be best in my case.

Mama and Daddy, probably on Easter, in the 1960s.
They are standing in front of the little brick house they
built on seven acres with a creek and a stream.

Mama's Love

*D*addy had been gone for a few years when I started my newspaper column so readers never met him in real time like they met Mama. Daddy had a "hard growin' up," as say the mountain folks. He was pitifully poor and raised without a lot of love or guidance. His mama left when he was 12 and took his two sisters north to West Virginia, leaving him with a drunkard of a father who beat him without mercy. Years down the road, Pawpaw Satterfield would repent, find the Lord and straighten up into a fine man. But in the days of my daddy's boyhood, he was anything but good. He scarred forever the heart and being of his only son.

Daddy 'runned oft' when he could stand it no more and surreptitiously lived in the barns of unsuspecting farmers, until Uncle Oscar and Aunt Fairy Cannon took him in and finished raising him to manhood. It's amazing how a boy with no raising of which to speak turned into such a fine man. All anyone could say to explain it was, "The Lord had His hand on him." "Honest Ralph" is what many people called him because his honesty was legendary, no matter what it might cost him monetarily. His childhood, no doubt, haunted him so a hateful streak could rise up from time to time, but other than those momentary lapses, he was steadfast, honorable, honest, solid and always offered a hand to anyone in need.

Theirs was a marriage that never waivered in its solidness even when they disagreed or got downright mad at each other.

"That woman could drive a sober man to drinkin'," he grumbled from time to time while she would storm, "I could just pinch his head off sometime. He makes me so mad."

In the little country school in which I grew up, there were 31 of us who started first grade together and not one child in that class would ever know the pain of a parental divorce. Families stuck together through thick and thin. I never felt the safety of my world was threatened by a possible split of any kind because Mama and Daddy walked through life shoulder-to-shoulder and sometimes hand-in-hand but always, without fail, together. There is a scripture in the Bible that says, in layman's terms, that two are better than one. That when one falls down, the other can lift up. That was Mama and Daddy. I saw time after time.

I wrote a couple of columns about that love and commitment. Mama's death, as you'll read later, was completely unexpected. We had dinner together the previous night and, as we were driving home, she began a dissertation on how blessed and wonderful her life had been. She talked at length about how extraordinarily happy she had been down through the journey of life. "I've had everything I wanted when I was a little girl. Everything." A couple of years earlier, she had shared that sentiment, so I wrote about it. The story that follows is about a gift of love from Daddy to Mama.

Mama's Happy Life

Mama said the most wonderful thing recently. What she said is something I wish I could hear from the mouths of everyone I care about.

"I've had the best life," she commented in an out-of-the-blue statement. She smiled sweetly. "I know my time on earth is dwindling down but I wouldn't change not one iota about my life. It's exactly what I wanted."

Now Mama's life, on any scale of measurement, has not been grand. It has been as a simple as a cotton gingham dress. There have been few vacations, store-bought clothes or new cars. Her memories don't include any historical moments or out-of-the-ordinary adventures. It has been as mundane of an existence as any woman of the rural South could ever know.

Still, she has loved it and prized it mightily. What more can you ask?

She's had abundance of what everyone who lives the happiest lives have – she has known love as mighty as the Mississippi and as strong as the four winds that blow in unison.

"I married the love of my life and had him for 58 years. No woman has ever been loved more than me," she continued. "I know I ain't had no fancy life but I've had exactly all I wanted. I just wanted to be a wife and a mama and that's what the Good Lord allowed me to be. I've been blessed."

It brought me up short and reminded me that contentment lies in the heart and can be found in the simplest of lives.

"I'm proud for the life you have," she said. "But you couldn't be one bit happier than I've been all these years. And you know me. Basically, I just stayed at home and took care of things around there except for church on Sunday."

A while back, a longtime friend passed away. I had visited with him on his terrace shortly before death had plucked at his ear and summoned him. By accounts of earthly measurement, he was impeccably successful. His career had been stellar and he had shared generously with those around him.

But as death eased with certainty toward him, he had regrets.

"I've made a lot of money," he said with a shrug. "Now, I'm leaving it for the vultures to fight over. All that money can't heal my body or bring forth the peace of a satisfied man."

My eyes watered as I studied the regret and disappointment in his faded eyes. I knew he had spent years chasing success as a way of covering up for the personal happiness he neglected.

"What's your biggest regret?" I asked because we were close enough that I knew he'd tell me. In fact, I felt he needed to get it off his chest.

He swallowed hard and looked away, focusing on a hawk that coasted lazily through the blue sky. He sighed and I could hear the heartbreak in that deep breath. "I let the woman I love get away. Pretended it didn't matter. That as long as I could make money, I could have anything I wanted on earth and be happy." He shook his head. "What a fool was I."

I wanted to cry, but for his downtrodden sake, I didn't. He turned his eyes to me. "Now you listen to me: don't let that happen to you. Nothing's more important than love. No amount of money or success can equal it."

Funny, but that's exactly what Mama, in her own way, said, too. While my friend couldn't take his money to the grave, Mama will take that love with her. And, she'll find more of it waiting for her on the other side.

Good choice, Mama.

The Windmill

From the moment I saw it, I thought it was the dumbest thing I'd ever seen. I spent 20 years thinking that, too.

"Whatta ya think?" Daddy stepped back, folded his arms across his chest with the look of a satisfied, proud man.

In typical teenager form, I rolled my eyes rudely and sniffed imperiously.

"Daddy, whoever heard of putting an ugly, old windmill in the yard – the front yard – of a modern brick house? It looks awful."

He should have popped me right then and there. But, instead, he turned to me, the smile dripping from his face and sliding to the ground, and said, "Little girl, one day you'll see things differently."

At 15, I couldn't imagine that I'd ever see things the way my daddy did. He was quare – in the words of his Scotch-Irish people – meaning peculiar in his ways.

For instance, we had a pasture fence that surrounded three sides of our yard. Daddy decided that by adding a chain-link fence to the front with a gate, he could extend the pasture and, therefore, board more cattle. Plus, if the cows ate it, he didn't have to cut it.

Many afternoons, I arrived home on the school bus to find the gate closed and a dozen or more registered Herefords grazing in our front yard, some lifting their tails and unceremoniously dropping dark remnants as my classmates watched.

I thought surely I would never live through the humiliation. But the worst was yet to come.

On the day I stepped off the bus and saw my simple-minded aunt, her childlike qualities brought on by a fever at age three, chasing my toddling niece up the gravel driveway while dodging the cows and their droppings, I wanted Jesus to take me home right then and there.

Aunt Josie's hair stood straight on end as if she had stuck her finger in the light socket and snuff dribbled out of the corner of her mouth and down her chin. I will admit, though, that she had on the cleanest, whitest Keds that I had ever seen.

So by the time that the windmill arrived, I had had enough. Daddy, though, wasn't relenting. He probably thought that repeated humiliation would make me stronger in life. It did.

I didn't know until many years later that the windmill had been a gift of love to his sweetheart. Mama, boosting his ego, had commented sweetly on a windmill he had added to the farm where he grew up.

"I wish I had one in my yard," she said, not meaning it at all. So, as soon as he could locate another one, Daddy bought a 30-foot tall windmill and plopped it in our yard.

What woman would want diamonds when you can have a windmill?

Over the years, I began to have appreciation for the

windmill. I saw it as lovely folk art. It is quite majestic with the weathered red blades and the blue tail that spins it around. It's not dumb. It's a unique monument to one man's love for his wife.

I built a house up the hill and across the river from Mama's and though there are trees between us, amazingly, there is a clear view of that windmill – beautifully framed by hardwood trees that surround it with green leaves in warm months, stunning color in the fall and raw limbs or an occasional snow in the winter.

I am awed by it.

Mesmerized, I will stare at it from my favorite chair through the living room window or sip morning coffee at the triple window in the dining room and admire the mist hovering around it. From the balcony outside my office, I often take photos in its various states of season and position. And, always, I sigh with appreciation.

For the time has come that I do, indeed, see things differently.

Mama's red pin cushion. Her skills as a seamstress
made enough money to put me through college.

Mama's wisdom
and her nosiness

$\mathcal{M}$ ama loved to give advice. Whether you wanted it or not. To be fair, though, outside of her children, most people really did want and treasured Mama's advice. Mama ran a little sewing business in the spare bedroom at our house. She started this when I was about 11 because she wanted to "make a little spending money so I don't have to ask Ralph for everything."

Not only was Mama a talented seamstress, one who could eye a dress in a catalog or store window then copy it perfectly, she was a remarkable business woman. She kept composition books that she called "my sewing book" and in it she listed the complete measurements of all her customers. Then, when they ordered something to be made, she listed it in the book. Dresses were $25, pants and shirts were $15 and skirts were $10. She so carefully managed her sewing money that she single-handedly paid all my tuition, books and other school costs which enabled me to graduate with two bachelor degrees from an expensive women's college.

Astoundingly, she allowed customers to open credit accounts with her. So, there in that book, also, she kept a running account of how much was owed and when payments were made on it. No one ever stiffed her on an account or had a returned check. No matter how long it took, they paid her off. A couple of years into the sewing business, Mama branched out to have fabric as well. She would search for deals then sell the fabric at a markup. Mama was disciplined about working in the sewing room. She began no later than 10 a.m., which gave her time to cook a hot breakfast, clean the kitchen, wash the dishes and make the bed. She worked until 12:30 p.m., when her program came on. For many years that was *Search For Tomorrow,* but when that ended, she moved on to *As The World Turns.* She had coffee and a sandwich then headed back to work. When the afternoon newspaper arrived, she took another break to have coffee and read it from front to back. She finished her day around seven then fixed supper.

"Idle hands are the devil's workshop," she said often. She lived by those words. She would sit in the den with Daddy and me every night, doing her "finger work" on a customer's order or family pieces. She sewed on buttons, hemmed or whipped down the inside facings. Whenever she was caught up on custom orders, she would make up dresses or outfits out of the fabrics she had for sell. Truth be told, in the 30 years that she sewed for others in that spare bedroom, she probably never cleared more than $30 for an item. But Mama was a smart money manager and she practiced the most important rule of economics: You spend less than you make. It's astounding how far she stretched her money and what a nice nest egg she had when she died.

That little sewing room was also a counselor's office. Many of the women who bought dresses from Mama sought her advice as well. They always needed someone to talk to and she was always there with solid advice and the kind of wisdom that helped to save our mountain folks from perishing. Mama's people knew how to live off the land, how to follow the signs of the moon for planting, harvesting, doctoring, predicting when babies would come and how to rightly sum up a person's worth. The King James Bible and the Almanac were their sole compasses for surviving life. They were, without question, mountain wise.

The story, *The Moon and The Pacifier*, is one example of Mama following the signs of the moon. Before she had her heart surgery, she sent Louise home to check the calendar and make sure that the signs were right for chest surgery. They were, so she proceeded. *Mama's Advice* is a story of a young man who worked part-time for me for years as he worked his way through school and how much he sought Mama's counsel. Eight days before she died, Brandon and I had gone over to have a hot, home-cooked lunch. It was getting toward the end of February, so we had spent the day outside, beginning an early spring cleaning of a winter's dreary yard. I finished lunch and went back to the yard to work on an embankment that is the bane of my existence. Brandon wanted to talk to Mama for a few minutes. "I'll be right there," he said as I left.

It was a long time before he returned. It was well over an hour and I was getting aggravated. Finally, he pulled up in his truck and jumped out with a big grin on his face. "That is the smartest woman," he said. "She was giving me advice on my love life. She's got some strong opinions on this girl I'm dating." He paused. "And, I think she's right."

When Mama died a week later, I thought back to that day and how that turned out to be her last counseling session with Brandon. When I called to tell Brandon, who was at college, of what had happened, he sat down, stunned. He said, "No, no. She can't be gone. I need more of her wisdom." Brandon was one of her pallbearers, tears running down his cheeks as he helped lift the handmade pine casket and carry it out of the church. *Mama's Advice* is a column I wrote about Brandon and Mama a year before she died. It is a credit to him that, at such a young age, he could appreciate her wisdom while admiration is owed to Mama for never failing to invest in others and for sharing her common sense approach to life and its challenges.

The Moon and The Pacifier

When my niece, Nicole, decided 'twas time to separate Zoe, who was nearing the age of two, from her pacifier, she consulted the lunar calendar.

In other words, like the wisest of Southern women, Nicole wanted to make certain that the signs of the moon were most beneficial for easing her child and herself through such a traumatic event.

See, such delicate situations should only be handled when the moon is in agreement. Taking a pacifier away from a child on the wrong signs of the moon would be the opposite of heaven. Nicole studied the signs. There were five days – from the eighth to the 13th – when the signs were right. This meant that the calendar, obtained from the local funeral home, showed the moon being in the legs. It's kinda complicated, but being the less than brilliant writer I am, perhaps I can explain somewhat succinctly.

In a lunar month, the moon travels from the head

down to the feet. A lunar-appropriate calendar will show when the moon resides in the head, then the neck, then the chest and downwards. When something needs to happen in one part of the body – in this case the mouth – the moon needs to be settled in the body as far away as possible. Nicole determined when the moon was in the legs and feet, circled those days in red and planned her course.

Zoe was about as attached to her "paccie" as my dachshund, Dixie Dew, is to a pork chop bone. In other words, nothing should come between either. Zoe had always been adamant about one thing: No paccie, no sleep.

But being the confident Southerners we are and believing in the signs of the moon like we do, we had faith that the lunar calendar that had served us so well for many generations wouldn't fail us now. After all, we had depended on it to see us through surgeries with record-time healings, garden plantings that produced abundant harvests and even cutting our hair when we wanted to make sure it grew slower rather than faster.

More than one dentist or doctor – oh, those scientific types – have laughed or rolled eyes when one of us said, "Let me consult the signs of the moon before I schedule that surgery."

The truth of the matter is that when the signs are right, there will be virtually no bleeding at the incision and the dryer the wound, the quicker the healing with no problematic infections.

Back to Zoe. We believe firmly in the lunar calendar, but we also have ample respect for an independent, stubborn toddler who, at such a tender age, is already set in her ways.

But the lunar calendar again rose to the occasion.

When Zoe arose from her nap one afternoon, Mama took the pacifier from her mouth, hid it in her diaper bag and then in her most artful way, weaved an engrossing tale of how she had thrown the pacifier out and the dogs had gotten it.

Zoe thought this was deliciously funny and giggled with great enthusiasm.

"Tell Ronda what happened to your pacifier," Mama instructed Zoe, whose mouth was covered in chocolate pudding.

"Dogs! Dogs!" she chanted, then threw back her head and laughed from deep in her little round belly.

And that was that. No pacifier. No tears. No problems.

It was amazingly effortless. So much so that Nicole called a friend who had battled twice before to take her baby off the bottle to no avail.

"Now's the time," Nicole announced. "Take it from him now. The signs are right."

In a snap of the fingers, the baby gave up his bottle. Another happy mama.

It's not easy to separate your baby from something she loves. Do you suppose there's a sign of the moon for taking a pork chop bone away from a chubby dachshund?

Mama's Advice: You Can Take Or Give It Away

Occasionally, I'll send Brandon, the nice young man who helps me out around the house, over to Mama's to do errands or yard work for her.

He loves her.

"Your mama is the smartest woman in the world," he

declared one day after a visit with her. He caught himself immediately. "Except for you, of course. I can tell where you get all your smartness. I just love to talk to her. She gives the best advice."

Now, this is just what Mama's been wanting and probably praying for – someone who actually thrives on her advice.

"Well, I'll tell you what," I said to Brandon. "You can have *my* share of her advice."

Fine and dandy with him. So the next time Mama started to offer her unsolicited opinion to me, I held up a hand for her to stop. "Don't start," I said. "I gave Brandon my share of your advice so you need to call him and give it to him. It would be unfair for me to take it after I gave it to him."

Another friend is a big fan and supporter of Mama's. One day he stopped by to see me, and Mama just happened to be at my house. He was delighted and rushed right over to hug her. Then, with one arm around her shoulder while casting an evil eye in my direction, he said, "I just wanted to tell you how sorry that I am that you have such a mean daughter. It's terrible how she writes about you."

Mama nodded and said, "I thought I had raised her better than that."

I shook a finger in his direction. "You just wait. If you stick around long enough, your time will come. Trust me. No one escapes Mama."

The other day his time arrived and I couldn't rush to the phone fast enough to call him and break the news.

"I love him like he's one of my own children," she said over lunch. Then she proved it by what she said next.

"But I'll tell you that something bad is wrong with him.

He's so unhappy in his eyes. It's showing up in age all over his face." She shook her head woefully.

Quietness overtook him when I relayed the conversation and you can be assured that he wasn't singing the praises of Mama. Yet another voice had been silenced by Mama's sharp tongue.

I sniggered. "Welcome to my world."

"I still love her," he said.

She went with me to a luncheon the other day. When I picked her up, she said, "I've spent all morning getting ready."

"I got ready in 30 minutes, including washing my hair," I replied.

She glanced at me. "And it looks like it, too." She paused. "You know I liked your hair much better back when you used to actually comb it."

Before I gave my share of Mama's advice away to Brandon, I actually gave her brief control over my life. All the decisions I was making on a particular situation weren't working so I figured I had nothing to lose by following her counsel.

"This is the chance you've been dreaming of," I told her. "You just tell me what to do and I'll do exactly what you say."

"Really?" She was incredulous and rightly so.

"Absolutely."

She hesitated, studying on it for a moment. "Now, I don't know that I want that responsibility."

"Oh no, you can't do that. You've wanted to run my life for years. Here's your chance."

So, she gave me her advice, I followed it to the letter and it failed worse than when I was running my life.

After that, I now say when she starts commentary on

the shape of my life, "Don't do that. I let you run my life once and you did worse than I do."

She smiled sinisterly. "But I plan to keep trying 'til I get it right."

And so it goes.

"White Lily flour is the best," Mama said. That's the bread basket she used for 60 years and her red napkin. I made the biscuits by hand just like Mama taught me.

Mama the Cook

Mama, owing primarily to her upbringing, was serious about cooking and was especially adept at big, hot breakfasts. This was the way that country and mountain people did: the woman of the house cooked a substantial breakfast and then dinner (called lunch elsewhere) to sustain the folks working in the fields. Traditionally, as soon as breakfast was finished, dinner was started, finished and waiting on the table at noon sharp. After everyone had finished, a tablecloth was placed over the leftovers which were eaten for supper.

Every morning of my childhood, teenage and college years, I awoke to the aroma of bacon or sausage. Daily, Mama made a pan of buttermilk biscuits, scrambled eggs, fried a breakfast meat of either country ham, sausage or bacon and finished it off with an iron skillet of creamy sawmill gravy made with full milk or 'sweet milk' as Mama and Daddy always called it. Sometimes, if she had fried up country ham, she made red-eye gravy by taking the ham grease and stirring it together with hot water and coffee. It is delicious poured over steaming grits. They both finished off the hearty meal by pouring sorghum syrup into a small plate, mashing butter in it then spreading it over one of the remaining biscuits.

When I was about three, Mama started sharing her coffee with me. It had a good dose of milk and a couple of tea-spoons of sugar. When I was four, a morning I remember distinctly, I pushed back my eggs scrambled with sausage and doctored thickly with home-churned butter, and said, "I'll just have coffee." From that day forward, I refused any of the hot, delicious breakfast food Mama cooked, and drank coffee only. Every morning, beginning in the first grade, I would pull myself from the bed, wash my face then stumble into the kitchen where Mama had my coffee, fla-vored with cream and sugar, waiting for me on the kitchen table. I picked up the cup, went back to my bedroom and sipped my coffee as I dressed for school. It didn't bother Mama a bit that she was sending her child off to school with no nourishment other than coffee. I loved this about her. I also loved that I never had a bedtime. I could stay up as late as I wanted, but if I fell asleep in the den while watching TV, she made me get up and go to bed immedi-ately. I often stayed up until the 11 p.m. news came on, a fact that astonished my first-grade teacher when she queried each child on what time we went to bed. Almost without exception, each said "Nine," and she smiled her approval. Upon learning the terms of my nightly surrender, she did not hide her disapproval.

"You mean to tell me that you don't have a bedtime?"

"No ma'am."

"Your parents allow you to stay up until the late news comes on?" She eyed me suspiciously while the rest of the first class looked at me with eyes full of admiration and envy.

"Yes ma'am."

She pushed her horn-rimmed glasses back on her nose. "Are you telling a fib?"

"No ma'am. You can call my mama and ask her."

I suppose when I offered that, she realized that the truth was, after all, in me. She pursed tightly her lips neatly painted in deep red lipstick – surely Revlon's famed Cherries in the Snow – and shook her head. She never seemed to care much for me after that, an assumption that edges closely to the truth when I recall the notes she hand-wrote on my report cards such as "does not play well with others," and "talks too much."

Despite the fact that I was undernourished and sleep deprived, I had the happiest childhood possible. All photos from that era show a little red-headed, freckle-faced child bursting with joy in her eyes and laughter in her smiles. It was a childhood filled with books, mud pies, dogs, television and long, dreamy, barefooted summers of blackberry-picking, games of pretend and wading in the tree-shaded creek. My happiness, no doubt, was aided by an easy-going mother who was mostly concerned with what I wore to church and how I acted when out in public. She had already raised three children so she had the nonchalance of a woman who, in mid-life, found herself with yet another baby, one unexpected, and decided she wouldn't worry herself to death about small matters.

I did not, to my everlasting regret, grow up on a diet of Cokes, potato chips and candy. The only junk food treat of any duration was the orange or cherry Kool-Aid that I was allowed to inhale during the summer months. At a Tupperware party, when I was 10, Mama bought a sectioned plastic container that allowed her to make popsicles from Kool-Aid. It was wonderfully exotic. For the most part, though, I was relegated to homegrown vegetables, farm- raised meat and either freshly made biscuits or cornbread at every meal. My sweet tooth was satisfied by biscuits covered in butter and sprinkled with sugar or chocolate gravy poured over biscuits. No one ever came to Mama's house without being offered food and usually she insisted on it.

"It won't take me but a minute to stir somethin' up real quick," she'd say, grabbing her apron and heading with solid purpose toward the stove. No one ever came to work at her house without being fed a huge lunch.

Once, after a crazy day of running endless errands, I returned home to find a message from Mama on my answering machine.

"I cooked dinner for the painters. I thought you might want to come over and eat." I had just had my house painted then sent them over to Mama's to paint the overhang and porches.

Here's the translation for that message: "cooked" means "feast"; "dinner" means "lunch"; "painters" meant that Mama was feeding the hired help again.

That was nothing new.

She'd been doing that as long back as I can remember, back to the days when Daddy sent men out to build pasture fences, get up hay or do any other work around the house.

Just a couple of weeks earlier, Mama had cooked up a huge meal for the men who were putting in a new central heating and air system at her house. This is a throwback to a world that few know now, a world where anyone standing on your property when mealtime rolled around got a hot meal and a glass of sweet tea. Though Mama grew up poor in the Appalachian foothills, they shared whatever they had. Normally, all they had was a bit of food, but they never held back a morsel.

I called her back. "What do you have?" I asked when she answered. Not that I was planning to go. I was just being nosy.

She was standing in the kitchen, surveying the bounty as she called it off. "I've got chicken casserole – and it's real good, too – fried chicken, candied yams, creamed corn, mashed potatoes, green beans, fried okra, hot biscuits and gravy and a fresh peach cobbler."

"You don't cook like that when I come over," I said dryly.

"You don't work when you come over," she retorted. That wasn't necessarily true but we won't go into that.

Since the painters, who were at Mama's, were the same ones who had recently been at my house, I said, referring to the head painter, "I bet Richard's tickled to death."

"I don't know," she replied, slamming the refrigerator door. "I don't know which one is Richard."

Only someone of my mother's generation would spend all morning in the kitchen, cooking a feast for men who were nameless to her. Richard spoke up, his mouth obviously full.

"That's me! Tell her that I read in her column that when you go to Mama's house, you have to eat. She was right! Yum-yum!"

Mama took great joy in all the bragging she got for these kind of meals. For a period of time, a few years before she died, she cooked for the family on Thursday nights and on the occasions that she found bacon on sale for a good price, she'd stock up and call all of us to say, "I'm cookin' breakfast for supper. C'mon over and eat." From wherever we were, we scrambled because nothing could beat Mama's breakfast cooking especially after she mastered the art of making perfect, boiling hot cheese grits.

Quite astonishingly, I have become a good biscuit maker. No one was more surprised by this than Mama. As you will see in the story that follows, I made up my mind I was going to do it and I did it. But, to be forthcoming, I had watched Mama for years make her daily batch. Mama never rolled out her dough. She made it in a big bowl then pinched it off, rolled it quickly in her floured hands and put it on the greased pan. "Making biscuits out by hand" is what the old-timers say. That is the way I make mine. Though I used Martha White Flour for years, I finally succumbed to Mama's advice and moved to White Lily flour. I have to admit that I was probably partial to Martha White because the brand sponsored the Grand Ole Opry for many years.

"White Lily's the best," Mama said.

"Why?" I asked.

"It just is." Though Mama couldn't explain, I did some research and discovered that the process used for milling White Lily makes a lighter flour and a fluffier biscuit. The top Southern biscuit makers recommend White Lily. Intuitively, Mama chose the best flour.

In the first column that follows, Mama is proud to learn that I can make biscuits. In the second one, she is irascible over a new soup recipe that I tried.

From One Biscuit Maker to Another

They are words that every decent Southern woman hopes to hear from her mother.

My mama said 'em but I never thought I'd hear 'em.

She bit into one of the crisp, buttered biscuits delivered to the kitchen island directly from my oven. I saw the look before I heard the words. It melted over her face like the butter melted across the top of the hot buttermilk biscuit when I pulled them out of the hot oven.

"Hmm." She savored another bite. "These are the best biscuits I've ever tasted."

I grinned from ear to ear. She stopped chewing and looked at me suspiciously. "I didn't even know you could make biscuits. Where'd you learn how to do this?"

The rest of the family dug into the fresh-baked batch, all affirming their deliciousness and each echoing Mama's sentiment with various refrains of "Where did you learn to make biscuits like this?" They were astonished.

It's quite simple. I got serious about the art of Southern biscuit making. After all, if you're going to be a Southern woman of the highest possible caliber, you've got to know how to make great buttermilk biscuits.

I have studied it prodigiously or, as Mama would say, I just set my mind to it. I realized the vast importance of Southern biscuit making when I watched a public broadcasting documentary, first broadcast in Nashville, called *The Rise of The Southern Biscuit*. Now, you know that Southern biscuits are of monumental national importance when PBS is doing an entire documentary on them. This is serious stuff.

At the Margaret Mitchell House in Atlanta, I bought the PBS documentary and began my thesis on the subject. Then, I turned to the next most notable authority on Southern biscuits – Martha White Flour. I dug out a recipe book that the Martha White folks had given me a few years ago when we did a book event together in Birmingham. I studied every word.

Next, I took the newly acquired information, turned my kitchen into a test kitchen and set about becoming an accomplished biscuit maker.

My primary education began in Mama's kitchen, a good starting place since the woman has made thousands of biscuits in her lifetime. Two things she taught me: To have the lightest, fluffiest biscuits, work the dough quickly and make them out by hand. Rolling the dough and cutting them out makes for a slightly tougher biscuit.

So, I flour my hands, pinch off a piece of dough, roll it quickly once or twice in my hand then pat it into the greased pan.

The other day when Mama was sick with a stomach ailment, I took her a small batch of biscuits, hot from the oven. After all, nothin' says lovin' like a hot biscuit. She called the next day.

"You haven't made any biscuits today, have you?"

"No."

"I've eaten every one of those. They're delicious. How do you make those biscuits so crisp and browned so perfectly on both sides?"

It's thrilling when your mama, who's so good at something, asks for your advice. I launched into a dissertation.

"You have to leave a quarter of an inch between the biscuits to have crisp ones. If you press them together, they won't be crisp. And, too, Martha White says to bake them at 425 degrees. You bake yours at 500 degrees. I've baked them at both settings. You'll always have a better biscuit at 425. But it'll take about 25 minutes to bake."

I was on a roll. I wasn't stopping.

"Five minutes before they're finished, I pull 'em out, put butter on the tops and poke a hole into 'em so the butter can melt down into the biscuit. Put 'em back in the oven." By the way, I figured that one out by myself.

Mama listened indulgently then commented, "Oh, I just thought you had a perfect oven."

Well, that too.

The Matter of Family Manners

Karen and I exchange recipes often. She's an excellent cook so I can always count on her recommendations.

Except for the tortilla soup recipe she passed along. It was okay, but not particularly enticing. However, as is often the case when I cook something, I'll call Mama and say, "I'm bringing you supper." I took her a carton of soup, dressed up with cheese, tortilla chips and sour cream then placed it on a tray and handed it to her as she sat contently in her easy chair, watching the evening news. This is the kind of treatment that every mama, after years of diapers, stomach aches and heartaches, dreams of having.

"Oh good!" she exclaimed cheerfully, clapping her hands together like a small child. She spread her napkin, spooned up the steaming mixture and put it to her lips. Then, also just like a child, her face crumbled into the ugliest mess of disgust you've ever seen. She looked like she was swallowing castor oil.

"What's wrong with it?" I asked because there was no need to ask whether she liked it or not. That was evident.

"It's got some kinda spice in it that I don't like."

"Then don't eat it." Commonsensical advice, I thought.

"If I don't, what'll I eat?" She cut her eyes over at me. "But it ain't good."

I sat on the sofa and watched as she took a few more pained bites. She didn't even try to hide the fact that she hated it.

"Honestly, Mama, I'm sure that Jesus didn't react half this bad when He drank the vinegar. I'm going home. I can't watch this production anymore."

Now, before you think too bad of Mama for not hiding her disgust over a supper that I cooked and delivered to her, know this: I have acted that way with her many times over the years of my life. Not too long ago, she insisted – that is she badgered, persisted and harangued – that I eat some collard greens she had cooked and drenched in some kind of hog grease.

"They're good for you. You need 'em for your digestion and to give yuh iron."

I took one bite and shuddered all over. "Yuck!" I stuck my tongue out, dramatically trying to shake the taste off of it. "That is awful." The only difference between Mama and me is that I didn't keep eating them.

But that brings me to today's thought: Why is that we – especially the well-mannered, thoughtful Southerners we are – treat our own families with such a lack of courtesy at times? Had either of us tasted anything cooked by someone outside of the family and disliked it, we'd both hid our disgust. And to be honest, I would have even lied about it, saying something like, "Hmmm. That's nice."

Mama, though, wouldn't have lied. You probably knew that, though. You've witnessed her straight-forward honesty many times in this column. She would not, however, made such an ugly face and she simply would not have said anything.

Isn't it a shame that we, as a well-mannered society, treat our families the worst? Mama will say things to me that my biggest enemy wouldn't think and I'll pop back with something that is tinged with just a bit too much hatefulness.

These are the people who love us – or so it is rumored – unconditionally. Yet, we think nothing of saying hurtful things or dispensing with niceties like thank you notes or even a spoken word of appreciation.

As usual, I called Mama the next morning to check on her.

"Did you sleep good?" I asked.

"No, I had heartburn all night. Nearly killed me."

I'm no longer offended.

Then she added. "But you did a real good job mixing it all together. Normally, you're not a bad cook."

"Thank you," I replied, recognizing the embedded compliment.

Please notice that we're working on our manners. Thank you.

Mama's favorite recipe for chocolate cake is stained
with chocolate batter, torn and held together with
pieces of silver duct tape.

Birthday Wishes

Is it possible that I am the only person whose mother annually forgot her birthday? You would have thought if anyone was going to remember that it would be my mama. After all, she told the story over and over of the surprise she and Daddy got when they discovered she was pregnant.

"On my 40th birthday, I said, 'Well, they say life begins at 40. We'll see.' And it did. Your life began when I was 40." She beamed. "You weren't planned but no baby has ever been wanted more. Your daddy was beside himself, he was so happy." When I arrived on that bitterly cold January night, I joined a family of siblings who were 18, 15 and 11 years old.

"We had one in diapers and one in college," Mama often chirped.

My birth should have been memorable if for no other reason than I arrived less than three hours after Daddy, calmly, escorted Mama into the hospital. She had seen the doctor that Friday afternoon and Doc Walker said, "Stay in town. This baby is gonna to be born soon." So, rather than going 15 miles home, she went to Aunt Ozelle's house, which was only four or five miles from the hospital. There, she was joined by Daddy, where they had supper and enjoyed the company of Uncle Tom and Aunt Ozelle. Around

7:30 p.m., Mama's pains intensified. Half an hour later, she said, "Ralph, we better call Dr. Walker and go to the hospital."

"Let me finish watching *Gunsmoke* then we'll go."

When "Marshal Dillon" finished his week's corralling of outlaws and no accounts, Daddy stood up, smoothed his pants, picked up his hat and said, "Now, let's go have a baby."

In the nursery were six babies. Three of us would grow up to be lifelong friends. We grew up together, went to school together and today, we all live within three miles of each other. There are many reasons Mama should have remembered my birthday and, to give her credit, she remembered until I was grown and on my own. Then, she started forgetting. For years, I was terribly hurt then I was just plain mad. Especially since Mama adored being indulged for her birthday.

"I can't believe you can't remember my birthday," I would rage.

"I have too much on my mind. I can't remember everything," she'd reply.

"You have NOTHING on your mind except *Oprah*, *Dr. Phil* and taking an afternoon nap after you've read the newspaper."

She'd sulk-up like a bullfrog so we'd be mad together for a day or two. Finally, I just decided that it wasn't going to bother me again. As you will read in the column that follows, I found a solution and it worked perfectly. I highly recommend it in the unlikely event that your mother doesn't remember the day she birthed you.

Happy Birthday to Me

This year, I decided the birthday present I most wanted was not to get in our annual argument with Mama. So, I gave it to myself.

And I enjoyed it the best of any gift I've ever received.

See, every year my mother – this is going to surprise you – forgets my birthday. I know. I know. I don't believe it either. But it makes me mad and we wind up fussing because, mainly, she is completely unrepentant that she doesn't remember her baby's birthday.

She does, however, recall in great detail the night I was born, beginning with Daddy telling her they would go to the hospital as soon as *Gunsmoke* went off, and ending with all the pain and suffering she endured for my six-pound, seven ounce, 19-inch long entrance into this vale of grief and sorrow.

"Then I should think you would never forget the precise date of all that torture," I'll retort. Mama just shrugs. No words of rebuke faze her at all.

"Well, really, it wasn't all that hard," she said. "I was always good at havin' babies. Some women are built better for it than others. It got easier every time so you were my easiest baby to have. Maybe that's why I forget."

Last year was the worse. The florist called Mama, trying to track me down, to say they had a delivery for me.

"We knowed you had a new house but we didn't know if you had moved yet or if you were traveling," the delivery woman explained when she brought me the flowers. "So I called your Mama." Only in a small town would this happen.

"Is today Ronda's birthday?" the florist asked after a couple of minutes of chitchat.

"I don't know," Mama replied. "Is it?"

The delivery lady thought that was hilarious, but I didn't see one thing funny about it. So, I thanked her for the flowers, set them down on the counter then charged across the floor to the phone, called Mama and promptly got into a fuss.

But I discovered something interesting before my birthday arrived this year. Mama forgets my siblings' birthdays, too. I never knew that before, so self-absorbed as I am. I called my brother late on his birthday. He said, "You're the only one who's called."

I called my sister on hers. She said that only my brother and I had remembered.

Now, my other sister, Louise, doesn't have this problem.

She shrewdly has outmaneuvered the system. She sends Mama flowers on *her* birthday. It's a brilliant reminder. A bit tricky but brilliant, nonetheless.

"Why do you send Mama flowers on *your* birthday?" I asked before I figured out what was really going on.

"Because she carried me for nine months and delivered me," she responded, trying to make it sound noble and unselfish.

When Louise's birthday came around a couple of months before mine this time, Mama called me and asked,

"Did you know that today's Louise's birthday?"

"Yes. I've already called her."

"Well, you know, I didn't realize it was her birthday until I got the flowers she always sends me on her birthday."

Finally, the light came on.

It should be noted, though, that we all know better than to forget Mama's birthday. I'll admit that for the past few years I've set Mama up in the way that wives set up their husbands by making certain that they aren't reminded of anniversaries. By doing this, you can be completely indignant, insulted and throw a beauty of a conniption fit if the date is forgotten.

This year, I opted against that.

"Mama, my birthday's this week."

"I know." No, she didn't but I couldn't prove that so we couldn't fight about it.

The next day: "Karen and I are going to dinner tonight to celebrate my birthday."

"Is your birthday on Saturday?"

"Yes."

Saturday arrived and I called Mama. "Today's my birthday. Call me back and wish me happy birthday."

"Okay." So she called me back, as though it was all her idea, and said, "Happy Birthday!"

When the florist called again, Mama said, "I know why you're calling. It's Ronda's birthday!"

No fussing at all. What a wonderful present.

Happy Birthday to me.

The old leather box that held Mama's precious papers – birth certificates, social security numbers, wills, her daddy's obituary and a photo of a man who had once been kind to Daddy. It is bound by red elastic which Mama stitched together on her Singer sewing machine.

Mama's Book

The last column I wrote about Mama while she was still alive was one that I was forced to pull from the lineup before it could run. It was one of my favorites, but Mama died before publication so I decided it was appropriate not to run it and would be less confusing for readers. Years later, I decided to make it a Mother's Day column and run it in her memory.

Folks will sometimes ask how I am able to come up with so many stories to write. The truth is that I have such an abundance of tales that my column is often written two to three months in advance. When Mama died, this column was four weeks away from running and though I hated to pull it, there really was no choice.

As you will read, Mama had taken to the notion of writing a book. Her life story. She figured if I could produce a book and she produced me then she could produce a book, as well. It was a late autumn day, the kind where the sun radiates brightly, the air is perfect with no humidity and the trees glisten in golds, oranges, yellows and reds. Mama had the door leading to the porch from the den opened, so I came in, let the storm door close behind me and sat down on the sofa. Mama had a notebook in her lap and paused, pen in hand, when I came in. That's when she "lowered the boom," as she liked to say, and announced she was writing a book.

I laughed. Her dark eyes narrowed. She raised her hand and flung that crooked forefinger in my direction. "That's all right, little girl, you laugh. But you can mark my words on this – ain't nobody ever had a better story to tell than I have."

When someone leaves your earthly life forever, you spend time thinking about them and what they did and how they did it. After her home-going, I pondered about Mama during long car trips, during a morning run, while cutting the grass or trying to fall asleep. With Mama, many things became crystal clear because my mind was no longer muddied by the kind of going-ons and carrying-ons that occurred while she was alive. A year or so before Mama had her heart surgery, she kept experiencing some chest discomfort and lack of energy. Since she had previously had a stint put in, we knew she had heart problems.

I called to check on her one morning and she was not improved, but not really bad off either. Still, I had an aggressive week of speaking engagements coming up and would be jumping from one plane to another. I made a plan.

"Okay, here's what we're going to do," I said, taking charge. Usually, my sister, Louise, took charge, so this was a rare change of command. "I'm coming over to get you and we're going to the emergency room. I have to leave in two days so we need to get this taken care of before I leave."

Mama didn't argue. This was a sign she was pretty poorly. She always argued when she wasn't all that sick. "Okay, I'll get dressed and be ready when you get here. I'll pack a gown and my hairspray." Louise was rather happy and pretty astonished to get the call that a new command had taken over the forces so she told me to keep her informed. Mama and I spent most of the day in the emergency room as they prodded, pricked, pushed, stuck then ran tests. We chatted, making observations about others in the ER and sometimes Mama dozed while I sat beside her and read. Mid-afternoon, a doctor appeared and said, "You've got a blockage and we need to put a stint in." Previously, when Mama had a stint put in, she had suffered terribly during the procedure. I figured that was on her mind so I took her hand. She smiled wanly.

"Mama, it'll be okay. Let's pray it won't hurt like it did the last time." I remembered clearly how they had rolled her out of surgery at Crawford W. Long in Atlanta and she turned her head from side to side, moaning, "I've never suffered so much in my life. It was terrible." They had a hard time getting the stint in. Of course, Mama tended to enjoy ill health and the attention it brought. Hundreds of times she had said, "I've never been so sick in my life. It's awful what I've been through." When Mama did not complain, it was always the red flag that she was really sick.

"We'll pray about it," I continued. Mama nodded. A serious thought crossed her mind and clouded her face.

"Ronda, promise me one thing."

"Anything, Mama."

"If anything happens to me, promise me that you'll go straight to my house and make my bed. Pick up the house and sweep. Don't let anyone in with it lookin' like it does now."

I threw back my head and laughed. She squeezed my hand tighter. "Promise me."

"I promise." Though it was good for a laugh in the emergency room, Mama was standing firmly on what she had always preached. Whenever our house needed dusting and mopping, Mama would say, "I tell you right now – this house is a shame and a disgrace. If somebody died and people had to come into this house lookin' like it does now, we'd all be disgraced."

This goes back to the days when the body was brought home to lay in repose. Still, whenever someone in our family dies, someone will say, "I'll go and clean the house."

After Mama died and I thought long and often about her life, I realized that Mama did have a powerful story to tell. Sometimes the most stirring stories rise up out of lives that seem ordinary but are anything but.

"Think about the courage it took for Mama to leave the mountains and go down to Gainesville and get a job," Louise said one day. "That was really something."

In the fall of 1937, Mama was 18 years old. They lived 15 miles from the nearest high school, so, with no way to get there, her formal education ended in the ninth grade of the one-room Nimblewill schoolhouse. She and her siblings walked two miles to school and home each day, regardless of weather. Mama loved schooling, though, so the teacher, Miz Estelle Lee, made special arrangements for Mama. She allowed her to come to school at the age of four and found lessons for her. When her other classmates left after the ninth year, Mama stayed on for another year or so until Miz Estelle had run out of things to teach her. That's pretty impressive.

A year earlier, a deadly tornado had laid to waste and rubbish much of the town of Gainesville, Georgia. Over 200 people had died and hundreds more were injured. The town was still in sad disrepair when Bonelle Miller caught a ride with a neighbor and rode up out of the holler then down the mountains to arrive 37 miles from where she started. For her, the journey was longer than any I have ever taken when I have flown across a few time zones. She left behind a four-room, tin-roofed house with a front porch that seemed to heave with sadness in a place so remote that they knew only what the weekly newspaper, the *Dahlonega Nugget*, told them and what they heard on a hand-cranked radio. Until she walked into her Aunt Nellie's house, she had never seen a room lighted with electricity.

She worked at Aunt Nellie's café for her room and board; then, a few months later, got a job at the hosiery mill making 18 cents an hour. In a short time, owing to the speed of her hands and her work ethic, she was raised to 25 cents an hour plus production (a bonus). She moved in with Aunt Alfie, Nellie's sister, and earned her keep at Aunt Alfie's boarding house by helping cook, serve meals and clean while continuing to work at the hosiery mill.

Though Gainesville was a small town of 10,000 people in 1937, it was a metropolis to a mountain girl whose nearest neighbors had been miles up the road and church services were their only social activities unless there was a barn-raising to be done. Now, she could window shop, go to a movie theater, visit with people and converse to learn about different lives and outlooks. She was always a social butterfly who was limited in the mountains. Now, she could flitter from one person to another all day long and never run out of people or conversation. Two years later, she met Daddy at, of all places, his river baptizing.

"I was dressed to beat the band," she said. "I had bought a burgundy suit and shoes and a hat to match. Now, I was somethin' to behold, I'll tell you that." She and a friend had gone back to the mountains for a baptizing. Mama was standing in the churchyard with her daddy when her eye was caught by a tall, handsome young man standing on the church steps.

"Daddy, who's that boy on the steps?" she asked.

He glanced around. "That's Ralph Satterfield. He's being baptized today. Why?"

Mama smiled. "Because that's the boy I'm gonna marry."

When they were introduced, Daddy took little notice of the well-dressed, pretty young woman. Mama, never deterred by much of anything, went back to her job at the hosiery mill and announced to her friends, "Girls, gather 'round. I have somethin' to tell you. I met the boy yesterday that I'm gonna marry."

It was well over a year before Bonelle heard again from Ralph, and when she did it was because one of the girls at the mill told her gleefully that a friend of hers "is dating that boy you said you were gonna marry." Ralph's girlfriend also worked at the hosiery mill. As far as Mama was concerned, that wasn't a dead end to her dreams. It was the beginning. He was standing right on the edge of her world. She marched over to the girl and questioned her about her courtship, then said, "Ask him if he remembers meeting Bonelle Miller."

After their next date, the girl returned to Mama and said, "He's not sure. He thinks he does but he wants to see a picture of you to make sure."

Mama had recently had a portrait made of herself so she sent one off to him that showed her with dark hair falling to her shoulders, a perfect, creamy complexion and remarkably straight, white teeth. Two weeks later, the handsome boy showed up on the porch of Aunt Alfie's enormous Victorian boarding house to see mama. He had remembered her all along but had pretended differently in order to get a photo. A year later, they married.

There are many stories that can be told from that point on, but one of the most important is simple yet powerful. Daddy went off to fight in the Pacific during World War II, leaving Mama with a beautiful, blonde baby girl. For two years, they did not see or speak to each other. Two years. A jagged string of letters often arriving two months or longer after being mailed kept them in touch. Somewhat. During those two years those two people did something extraordinary – they believed in, planned and worked for a better future. Daddy sent home every cent of every check. While on the ship, he cooked for officers and did their ironing to make extra money. At home, Mama took in sewing and cooking to make extra money. When Daddy returned, he discovered that Mama had saved every penny of his service pay because she and their little girl had lived on the money she made. Daddy took the savings and bought an Amoco gas station. For the rest of his life, Daddy would work for no man other than himself, answer only to God and he would always advise to "use white Amoco gas. It's the best there is."

So, in truth, Mama did have a wonderful story to tell, but back when she first told me, I wasn't so sure about it. But it became a column. I still smile when I read it.

Mama Writes A Book (Or Wants To)

My worst fears are about to be realized: Mama has announced her intentions to write a book.

My payback is coming.

Before the bombshell dropped, I was ruler of my own universe which means that I also reigned royally over Mama. I was completely in control of my little kingdom. Then in a matter of seconds, the bomb exploded and there was a changing of the guard. Suddenly, I was dethroned and the new queen supremely took her seat and my power was relinquished.

After a trip to the grocery store, we were, for once, driving along in silence. I was lost in my thoughts when out of the blue, Mama said, "I'm going to write a book."

It took a split second for the significance of that comment to sink in. When it fully hit me, it splintered my senses like a Louisville Slugger meeting a mighty top spinner. I jerked my head around. "What!"

She looked around calmly – see, this is how mighty kingdoms are tumbled in a single moment – and said, "I'm gonna write a book."

I started laughing. First, at what I thought was the sheer ridiculousness of it. Then, my laughter became a defense mechanism. After all, if I could convince her of the silliness of such a venture, she'd give it up. Right?

Wrong.

"I'm serious," she replied. She looked at me levelly, without flinching.

"What are you going to write a book about?

"My life. It's interesting."

"It's not *that* interesting." I was still on the offensive. I didn't realize that my seat time on the throne was growing shorter by the moment.

She shrugged. "I have good stories to tell." She smiled wickedly. "I have plenty about you I can tell."

This is when the offensive changed to the defensive.

"Me!" My eyebrows shot up and my mouth dropped. "You can't write about me."

Mama narrowed her eyes. This is always a serious sign. "You write about me all the time and half of it ain't true."

"All of it is true. And I have witnesses who can verify just about everything I've ever written."

"Don't worry, little girl, I'll be able to verify mine, too." Just for the record: When Mama calls me "little girl," the battle has begun.

I dismissed the idea and went merrily on my way. I did not realize at the time that my kingdom was in serious jeopardy. Then, I stopped by the house and found Mama settled comfortably in her easy chair, scribbling on a yellow, legal-sized notepad.

I eyed the pad suspiciously. "Whatta ya doin'?"

She grinned happily. "Workin' on my book."

Dismayed, I shook my head. I can only imagine my role in the book. I'm sure it won't be much of a pretty story for me. But to be honest, Mama is a good writer and a stronger storyteller.

"I have a title," she continued. "I'm gonna call it 'Mama.'" Oh great. Mama has now joined the ranks of Dolly, Cher, Elvis and all the other one-name celebrities. It's true, though, that strangers come up to her all the time and say, "Hi, Mama," or "How's Mama today?" We even have one friend who Mama has successfully diagnosed his ailments by using her beloved "doctor's book," and who now calls her "Dr. Mama."

I'm not sure what's going to become of this book, but I have heard some of the stories about me that she tells people and that leads me to only one conclusion.

At least for me, this book is not going to have a happy ending.

Mama Always Said

"Bad beginning, good ending. If it starts off bad, somehow it always winds up good."

My sister, Louise, and me with Mama during Christmas
sometime in the 1990s. We had a brother and another sister
but they missed being in most photos for one reason or the
other. Both of them have joined Mama and Daddy in
heaven's eternal realm.

The Christmas Story

In December before Jesus called Mama home in February, it was time to write my Christmas column. For a couple of months, I had been planning to write a wonderful story of Daddy's generosity and the good Lord's faithfulness. I wrote, it but another Christmas story, one that had influenced me deeply, kept tugging at my heart.

It was a story of Mama's kindness that I had witnessed at the age of four at McClellen's Five and Dime on the square in our hometown. It was a building with darkly rich, oiled floors and aisles of splendid trinkets. Though I was young, what happened that day had a deep impact on me and was one of the greatest lessons Mama ever taught me. It was the first time that I ever experienced a sentimental touching of my heart, the way you feel when a Hallmark commercial causes a misting of eyes. In her simple act, I saw kindness, compassion and generosity and that made my heart feel sad and glad at the same time. I remember it clearly.

Something was nagging at my heart to write that story but I already had my Christmas column written. I was burdened by the thought, so finally I decided to do what I've done only that once: I wrote two Christmas columns to run on consecutive weeks. I didn't tell Mama. I wanted her to be surprised.

As fate would have it, I stopped by Mama's on the day that the column ran in our local newspaper. Mama was sitting in her favorite recliner with the pages of the newspaper strewn beside the chair where she had dropped it piece-by-piece as she finished reading. The section with my picture, byline and column was laying on top of the pile. From my place on the sofa, I could read the headline and see that it was the one about Mama.

"Oh!" I said brightly. "Did you like the column I wrote about you? You're always wanting me to write good things."

"Yes," she said wearily as she rested her head against the back of the recliner. "It was good."

"I thought you'd be more excited."

She closed her eyes. "It was fine."

I didn't press the issue though I felt a bit letdown. Since Mama liked to be bragged on, I expected her to be beaming. But Mama was grieving. Her heart was broken for a reason I'll explain later. On top of the terrible sorrow she was experiencing, she was sick with pneumonia. She could barely hold her head up. Three times daily, I went to check on her, fixed her something to eat then made certain that she took the enormous-sized antibiotic pills that the doctor had prescribed. Her will for living was ebbing away. As she fought the sickness and sorrow, friends and family tried to love and uplift. When well-known or famous friends of mine called, sent a card or sent flowers, she was cheered tremendously. She kept a pad by her chair and would write down those names. One day I was there when a huge bouquet of flowers arrived from my dear friends Stevie and Darrell Waltrip, Darrell being one of the most famous drivers in NASCAR history. As soon as I read the card to Mama, she lighted up and grabbed her pad and pen.

"Oh, I've got to write their names down!" In my safe deposit box, I have that pad with those names written in her handwriting with the ink pen she used attached to it. I smile whenever I see it and remember her joy.

Mama taught me many things: how to cook, how to sew, how to sweep and mop, how to manage money, how to work hard and she emboldened me with many of her own wisdoms such as, "Be careful what you tell your best friend because she may not always be your best friend." The story that follows is the first lesson of the heart that Mama taught me. What a powerful lesson it was.

The Greatest Gift Is Teaching

At a Thanksgiving luncheon, I was holding my 18-month-old nephew, Tripp, as I visited tables to speak to folks. I stopped and greeted a friend, patting him on his back. Tripp watched quietly then leaned down, stretching out his little arm and patted Billy, too, in that awkward, uncoordinated way that babies have.

I chuckled, realizing that Tripp had simply emulated what he had seen me do. See, children are like that. They, more often than not, simply grow up imitating those they watch. Good or bad.

Every Christmas, I find myself imitating adults who used Christmas as a time of kindness and generosity. Last week, I mentioned that there are two particular Christmas memories that link arms and skip through my memory every Yuletide season. My heart always warms at thoughts of Daddy's many generosities, but mostly I am humbled by what I watched happen repeatedly, especially when he gave what he didn't really have to give. Amazingly, whatever he had given away came back to him many times over.

"You can't out-give God," Daddy always said. "Just try to out-give him." He'd wink in that smart aleck way he sometimes had. "I dare you."

So, each Christmas, I think often of that financially-bleak year when he had given away part of his property tax money because he found someone who needed it more than he. By that evening, God, not to be out given, had sent back the money in the form of business.

As much as I love that story from childhood, there is another that still moves me as deeply as it did the December afternoon that it happened when I was five. The memory is so powerful that it still easily coaxes tears from my eyes.

Remember dime stores? The predecessors to dollar stores? Mama and I were shopping a few days before Christmas in an old-fashioned one with ancient, unvarnished hardwood floors that were oiled regularly and creaked mightily. It was fascinating with its endless rows of trinkets and sparkling items. While Mama shopped for Christmas odds and ends, I wandered around the magical, dimly lit store until she called, "C'mon. I'm ready to check out."

Running my fingers across the edge of the display tables, I trailed behind her to the check-out. A young man, perhaps 17 or 18, was handing his merchandise to the clerk. There were a couple of costume baubles, a bottle of cologne and a scarf of which he seemed particularly proud as he tenderly handed it to the clerk. It was obvious, even to a child, that he was doing his Christmas shopping. I folded my arms, placed them on the counter and rested my chin there as I watched him. Excited, he waited as she rang it up.

"That'll be $4.87."

Carefully, he counted out dollar bills and change. Suddenly, panic sprang across his face. He didn't have enough.

"Oh no," he whispered. "That's all I've got."

The clerk shrugged. "Well, you'll just have to put somethin' back."

Tears welled in his eyes. He dropped his head.

"How much does he need?" Mama asked.

"Thirty-seven cents."

Wordlessly, she counted out the coins into the clerk's hand. Should the good Lord will me to live to 100, I shan't ever forget the look on that boy's face. He swung his head around and pure, heartfelt gratitude melted across his eyes. A million dollars would not have meant more.

"Thank you," he said softly, sincerely. Mama smiled and nodded silently. Bag-in-hand, he walked to the old wooden doors and pushed one open. He turned around and took one last smiling look at his angel and then he was gone.

Mama didn't see that last look. But I did. And I have never forgotten it.

Just as Tripp reminded me, children learn by watching.

Mama, Dixie Dew and me. We three enjoyed many
road trips together. Mama always babysat Dixie Dew
while I traveled. "She's the smartest one in the
whole family," Mama used to say, laughing.

Gone but still talked about

Mama cooked exclusively in cast iron skillets that had years of 'seasoning.' This is one of hers that she gave me when I started housekeeping. Like Mama, I use it all the time. I have two smaller ones for baking cornbread.

Turning into Mama

When Mama went home to be with Jesus, it became immediately clear that a huge void had just been created in our lives. Mama used to say, "This family has no idea how much I do for it. Where would all of you be without me? It's gonna be a sad day when y'all find out how much that Mama did, that y'all didn't pay one iota of attention to. Y'all are gonna miss Mama, I can promise you that. Mark my words."

Of course, at the time, we paid no nevermind to her but when that sad day arrived, we found absolute truth in that statement. We lost a dependable babysitter, one who fed the babies cheese grits from a generous-sized, blue-flowered cup, a seamstress that hemmed and altered anything necessary; a laundress who could miraculously get any kind of stain out of any fabric; a cook who was always willing to bake a cake or make deviled eggs when we didn't have time, a comforter who could encourage and pray during the difficult times and a voice of authority who always put in her two cents worth, whether it was wanted or not, or appreciated.

The worst part was that we had no backup plan. We had arrogantly believed that there would be no tomorrow that did not have Mama in it. We were wise enough to know that death is unpredictable in timing but always predictable in coming, yet we never focused on a future without Mama. Her death found us sadly lacking, and every day revealed a new way in which to miss Mama and remind us loudly of our loss.

A month after she died, my niece, Selena, needed a babysitter for her six-week-old baby, Tyla. Without Mama, she was forced to use her last alternative: me. No one in my family had ever entrusted a baby to my care, which shows just how bad things got. In fact, it got to the point that we all had to pool our abilities and talents to take up the slack. All told, it took four of us to fill the void created by Mama's departure. Mama was right – we had no idea how much she did for all of us.

As time passed, sometimes in a lamb-like gentle way, other times in the way of a roaring lion, I found myself becoming more and more Mama-like. I meddled way too much in the matters of my family, asserting my opinion as Mama would, beginning with, "Mark my words." I recycled plastic baggies that I washed out then dried, I made her special creamy, cheesy chicken noodle soup which I toted to anyone who was sick, I clipped coupons for the Pancake House and carried them in my purse. I pulled out the sewing machine and altered my own clothes; I toted buckets of bath water outside to pour on plants; and I began faithful forays to the funeral home. I even took to reading the obituaries on a dedicated, daily basis.

I wasn't the only one. My sister, Louise, and niece, Nicole, took on marked characteristics and traits of Mama, giving rise to the chiding, "Okay, Bonelle" evoking Mama's Christian name whenever one of us observed the other doing something just like Mama would have done or acting like her.

Slowly, we reached the conclusion that we were turning into Mama. Even the things that had driven us to distraction about her, the things we swore we'd never do, became a standard way of life for us.

"Oh my gosh," I said one day to Nicole. "We've all become Mama. Now we don't have just one Mama to deal with, we have three!"

Perhaps it was a way of keeping her alive, of taking her with us as we continued down through the journey of life. But more than likely, the woman who had raised us, the one who we then raised in her latter years, had instilled so much of herself deeply within us that it was a natural transformation. Her peculiarities became ours, her wisdom enlightened our decisions, her compassion softened our hearts and her quirks embedded themselves in our behavior, making us at times, peculiar and unreasonable.

In the end, we all, in some incarnation or the other, become the woman who raised us. If there is a finger to be pointed to the exact time when that happens, it must be the period in time when we daughters become the mother of our mothers and we take over raising them. That time when we fuss over them, fuss with them and fuss about them.

It is a fate that no woman can outrun or out-smart. Destiny, you see, arises in the raising.

We were left to carry on as best we could and, though we were not much good at it in the beginning, we got better. My readers were stunned and saddened with the loss of their favorite character. "No more mama stories?" they asked. I figured that I had some left to tell but that the stories would soon run their course. Nine years later, by the wit of Mama and the grace of the good Lord, I'm still telling new Mama stories. Since she never stopped talking, she left me with an abundance of stories. There are still many I haven't told so I'm sure it'll keep going for a bit.

During the eulogy at her funeral, I said to the congregation, "I bet y'all are all wondering if I'll have a career next week since Mama's gone." I paused and smiled. "But now I'm gonna tell the stories that I couldn't tell when she was alive!" The audience laughed and clapped. Everyone wanted Mama to go on and on.

Here's one of those never-before-told stories:

Mama never dated nor entertained the idea of a second husband. She loved her life and she especially enjoyed traveling with me and the newfound celebrity she had obtained. She switched off going to church with me, my sister Louise or my Aunt Kathleen and Uncle Delbert, who was Mama's brother. On the Sundays that she went with me, she was always happy for the adventure. I had taken to sitting with a gentleman who had many challenges in life. Sims's right arm was drawn up, his hand twisted and gnarled and his right eye drew toward his nose. One leg was noticeably shorter than the other and his foot turned in. Walking was a challenge and so was talking. Every word took effort but he always managed without help and even drove himself. He had both pride and determination. I was drawn to Sims and my heart loved him dearly.

One Sunday, he said to someone with a proud smile, "Of all the people she can sit with, she sits with ME." He loved me enormously and always brought me a caramel candy wrapped in cellophane. Like a hawk, he guarded my seat on the second pew near him. If someone threatened to sit there, he would squawk, "No! This is for my friend, Ronda. You can't sit here." Typical Baptist when you think about it.

Always sitting on the same pew in the seat next to the aisle was one of the most dashing, courtly Southern gentlemen anyone could ever have the pleasure of knowing. Mr. Turnkey was 88-years-old when I came to know and love him. He was a wealthy widower who had made his money as a wise businessman.

On the Sundays that Mama wasn't with me at church, Mr. Turnkey would spot me, smile beamingly and stand up to let me in so I could sit next to Sims. "Someone's been waiting on you, watching the door," he would whisper in my ear as he let me pass into the pew. Sims, for his part, was ecstatic. He would hug me, squeeze my hand and dig into his pocket to pull out the candy he had brought.

My friendship with Mr. Turnkey started primarily because of my friendship with Sims. "I have the greatest of admiration for you," Mr. Turnkey said one day. "You have no idea how much joy your kindness gives that young man." Well, Sims wasn't really "young". He was in his fifties, but when you're headed into your nineties, I suppose you see age differently.

This is how Mama came to know Mr. Turnkey. On the Sundays she was with me, Mr. Turnkey would rise gallantly and allow me to slide in next to the deliriously happy Sims. Mama sat next to me then Mr. Turnkey sat next to her. After several Sundays of this seating arrangement, I noticed that Mama and Mr. Turnkey were sharing a hymn book. She was 87 but acted 17. Coquettishly, she looked up at him, smiled flirtatiously and winked occasionally. The first time I saw it, I did a double take. Mr. Turnkey was responding with a youthful glint in his eyes.

One day we got in the car after church. Mama, smoothing her skirt, was flushed with happiness. Giggling, she said, "I want to tell you somethin' – Mr. Turnkey likes me."

I rolled my eyes comically and shook my head. "And, what makes you think that?"

"He asked for my phone number."

I nearly ran over the curb. "What?"

She giggled again. "And I gave it to him."

She was so happy that I started laughing. She turned and looked at me. "What would you think if I got married again?"

"Well, first, I think you're being a little premature about that but, second, as long as he can drive, I'm all for it." Mama had given up driving when she was in her thirties and had a fender bender. She always kept her license current and bravely fought to overcome her fear of driving when I was in the fifth to ninth grades, so that I could participate in after school programs like Camp Fire Girls, 4-H, FHA, Student Government and other activities. It was five miles to my elementary school from our house and eight miles to high school. It was a huge challenge for her so I will always be appreciative. Since we lived in the country and didn't have close neighbors, it was important in my socialization and development. As soon as I turned 16 and got my license so I could take care of myself, she never drove again. Ever. So she had to be taken for groceries, doctor appointments, shopping and church. Daddy took care of that until he became sick, then it fell mostly and abundantly to Louise and me.

Mr. Turnkey called Mama that night and thus began a friendship that slowly grew. After a couple of months, Mr. Turnkey asked Mama for a date. The church was hosting the seniors for a Valentine's Day banquet and he asked if she would join him. It had been 10 years since Daddy died and not once had she considered dating, saying, "Oh, I'm too old for any such."

But when Mr. Turnkey asked, she did not hesitate. "I would love that," she replied, trying to hold back some of her giddiness.

On the day of the banquet, she called me. Some things you never forget where you were when they happened. I was driving around a high-rise parking deck for an Atlanta hospital on my way to see a friend who had been critically injured in a car crash. "I need you to help me with what I should wear. I just can't decide. I don't think I should wear pants, do you?"

"No, wear a dress. This is your first date and you need to dress-up like a lady." I paused. "And make sure you act like a lady and don't embarrass me. I want folks to know that I raised you right." These were the words she often said to me before I left on a date. I was smiling broadly at her girlish anticipation. We decided on a red suit with an ankle length skirt. I wish I had a photo. Before Mr. Turnkey could ask for a second date, he got sick. Mama didn't hear from him for several days and, like most teenage girls, she was worrying about when or if he would call again. After a week of not hearing, Mama got in the car for church on Sunday with a big smile on her face.

"Guess what? He called." This went back to the days of my youth when a boyfriend had disappeared from sight and I had grieved. One night, I came in to find a note on my dresser from Mama. She had scrawled, "Guess what? He called." No note had ever made me happier.

"Mr. Turnkey?"

She nodded. "He's been terribly sick with the flu and

pneumonia. Oh, he sounded awful on the phone last night. I'm so worried. He's not eating but said he'd like to have some buttermilk."

"I tell you what – if you'll make him some cornbread muffins, I'll make him some of your chicken soup and I'll run it over to him after Sunday School." We were having a birthday party that afternoon for my dog, Dixie Dew, so I knew we'd have to hurry to get everything done in time.

"That's a wonderful idea!" We went to early service at my sister's church then I left Sunday School early. Mama, so healthy and happy, was waiting for me in the upstairs sanctuary. On the way home, we stopped at a little grocery store and bought all we needed. She picked out orange juice, a gallon of buttermilk and a peach pie for Mr. Turnkey, while I got the ingredients for the soup including the Velveeta cheese. I dropped Mama at her house to make the cornbread and I went home to fix the soup. An hour later, I picked up what she had for Mr. Turnkey and drove to his house in a gated community. She called to tell him I was on my way with the food.

When he opened the front door, it was obvious that he could barely hold up his head but he was so happy to see me and so grateful for the food. He beamed with joy. By the time I got home, he had already called Mama and thanked her. Three hours later when the doctor somberly told us that Mama was gone, one of my first thoughts was Mr. Turnkey. I couldn't call him. I couldn't break his heart like that. I called his pastor and asked the minister to break the news to him. It didn't matter who told him. His heart was deeply hurt.

The series of columns that follow are ones that have been written after Mama's death. As you will see, Mama stories are the gift that keeps on giving.

Guess What?

As life stretches on, it is always a blessing to share a history with those who know you well. It is a bond that cannot be fabricated for it is created by the times and stories you mutually share over many years.

Mama called one day. I was talking to my agent who said, "Do you need to get that?"

"No," I replied when I saw the number on caller I.D.

Then my cell phone rang and I was alarmed since she never called my cell. I quickly finished my conversation and called her immediately. When I heard the lilting, gleefulness of her voice, I knew something was awry.

"I have something I want to tell you," she gushed.

"What?" I asked warily.

"Guess what?" She paused then announced dramatically. "He came."

The moment I heard the words, I knew. My mind spun back many years to a broken heart and the endless days and nights when I had pined for him to call. It was always Mama's habit to give me my messages as soon as I walked in the door. That night, she said nothing and I, dejected after three weeks of no news, shuffled off to my bedroom. On my white French Provincial dresser was a note in Mama's sprawling handwriting: *Guess what? He called.*

It was probably one of the happiest moments of my life, the kind of unabashed joy for which we wish as we grow older. Somewhere, I have that note still.

"Guess what? He came," told me that the reason for that long ago heartache was sitting there in Mama's den. For some reason, my old boyfriends have always had more affection for Mama than for me.

"Are you serious? Is he there now?" For those kind of intricate bonds can speak in code, skipping the facts such as names.

She laughed. "Yes, he is. C'mon over and see us."

I settled down on Mama's sofa and smiled. "So, you must be out of anything to do if you've come here to visit."

He banged his head against the back of the rocker and rolled his eyes. "I knew you would say that. I knew it'd be the first thing out of your mouth. I predicted it."

Mama grinned and nodded. "He did."

I shrugged but couldn't resist a smile because it felt so right for all of us to be together in that den again, sharing our mutual stories of a time, mostly happy, so long ago.

"Do you remember that night that all Ronda fed you for supper was greens beans and cornbread?" Mama asked, cutting her eyes over at me. "We had gone to revival and I had a refrigerator full of food but she only gave you what I left on the stove."

And thus the stories continued for a while.

Later, that evening, I said to Karen, the best friend who has traveled the winding roads of those years with me, "Guess who came to see Mama today?"

She gasped. "You're kiddin' me! Really? Oh my, I remember how bad he hurt you." Then she began recalling some of the less-lovely details of the falling apart. And, to be quite honest, it was all his fault. Like the best friend she is, she, still after all the years, was indignant and protective. "It was terrible!"

But instead of feeling sad for that time long ago, a wonderful feeling crept over me.

"Isn't it wonderful that we share such a history?" I

asked, thinking not only of Karen but of Mama and him as well. "We go back so far that we know everything about each other. The good times and the tough ones."

I hung up the phone, remembering the man who broke my heart and the two women who had nursed me through it.

Guess what? I smiled.

Packing Up My Suitcases

Too often I used to stop by Mama's and find her with that look in her eye. I'd know it the moment I walked in, so I silently curse myself for picking that time to drop by.

It was a no nonsense look which warned me before she ever spoke not to cross her or dispute her.

She'd sigh wearily. "I've been cleanin' out this morning – I'm so worn out I can barely move – and there's a bunch of your stuff sittin' in the living room. I want you to take it and get it outta my way. You got more room than I've got."

It was usually junk. Not really worth keeping but too sentimental to discard. It's the kind of stuff that I preferred to keep at Mama's. But that not being an option, I loaded it up and dragged it home to my attic. One day, she'd been cleaning out the closet in the sewing room.

"Get that luggage and take it home or I'm gonna give it to the Salvation Army," she ordered.

That luggage – *that luggage* – is not going to the Salvation Army for it means too much to me. So I hauled that hot pink Samsonite set home with me and smiled as I packed it in the attic with four other sets of luggage, including a polka dot set, two pieces of genuine Louis Vuitton, a French made tapestry set (my first with wheels – God's greatest gift to a traveler) and the black and white mingled cloth of a Samsonite. My favorite suitcase – a compact leopard print wheeler – is in the hall closet because it is used almost weekly.

Earlier, as I picked up the hot pink luggage – and it is still a gorgeous color – I thought of something else.

"Do you know where that brown leather set of Samsonite is? The set we had when I was a little girl?" I asked Mama, the former Patron Saint of Storage.

"It's here somewhere and when I find it, you can take it, too."

"Good," I replied and I smiled when I thought of that one piece that was a childhood companion.

Driving home, I glanced over at the hot pink leather tote bag and I realized, for the first time, its significance. I was born to wander. I came into this world to roam, sometimes aimlessly, sometimes with great purpose. A sophisticated gypsy, a friend once said of me, pointing out that I am intrigued by the byways and backroads of this life and the things they teach me, the stories they whisper to me.

As early as five or six, I would drag the family suitcase – that brown leather Samsonite – from the closet, fill it with my little clothes then play for hours my pretend game of going to New York City on business about books. Honestly. How did a pre-schooler in the rural landscape of the South know that New York is the heart of the publishing industry? Destiny. It's that simple.

All children know at an early age where they are meant to go. It is as instinctive as breathing. Some follow that path. Too many, though, hindered by misjudgments, misguidance, mishaps or mistakes fail to take the calling of their childhood into adulthood. Then destiny is missed.

In junior high, I discovered that stunning hot pink luggage and yearned for it. Not that I had anywhere to go, for I only remember one family vacation. The summer I was 11, my parents and I took a two-week sojourn to visit family who had moved to West Virginia. It was beyond exciting. For two years, though, on birthdays and Christmas, I got a piece of that luggage until I had the full set. It is practically unused yet it was most useful.

I packed my dreams in there and set out to travel the path of my calling.

Becoming Mama

Now that Mama's gone, it seems pertinent that someone step up and take her place. Or try to, anyway. Regarding the kind of life that Mama had, I think I'd like to step up and volunteer to turn into Mama. Now, that woman had it made.

I think back to one afternoon when I popped in to see her. I plopped down in the rocker and wearily rubbed my brow.

"Whatta you been doin' today?" She was ready to have a good, long conversation.

"Don't ask," I replied. But because I'm a glutton for punishment, I poured out my story. I began with the financial institution that had made a serious mix-up, which resulted in endless calls between them and my accountant's office and segued into the clause in a publishing contract that was not clear and all the havoc that had wrought. Those were the high points. There had been other problems but they paled in the aggravation to what those first two had caused. I was completely stressed out.

Mama listened, and rather than offer a consoling word or a shoulder, she began her lecture. "This too will pass. You can't let these things get to you. You have to control your stress and resist pressures."

My eyes narrowed. "Coming from someone who rarely has any pressure in her life, your words are of little consolation. You have never had to deal with stresses like this so I'll pass on that advice."

Mama laughed and shrugged.

This is true. First, Daddy took care of Mama. When he died, Louise and I inherited her, so her pressures became ours. From grass-cutting to pharmacy errands to bank deposits to tax issues to doctor visits, we took care of it for her. My sister even visited weekly to do Mama's hair for her.

One Saturday, I happened in on them in the bedroom. Mama was situated there in front of the huge mirrored vanity while Louise curled, teased and sprayed. I leaned against the door frame and observed for a moment. I was curious.

"How did you ever get to be a grown woman without learning how to do your own hair?"

The Queen smiled grandly and shrugged. "I just never learned."

Well, see, there's the answer. If you don't learn how to do something, you don't ever have to do it for yourself. My friend Pat in Memphis claims she never learned to pump gas so every time she needs it, her husband takes her car for a fill-up. Stupidly, I've learned how to do too much.

But not Mama. She was smarter.

Whatever she needed, someone did for her. It was a wonderful life. She had the right idea, though. You can't blame the woman for that. I can't fault a woman who is smart enough to find others to do her bidding even if one of those doing the bidding is me.

"I don't want this call waiting on my phone," Mama said one afternoon when I was at her house. "You call and have it taken off for me." She didn't know how to use it anyway. All she knew is that if she heard a clicking noise while talking to someone, that meant another call was coming in. She'd say, "Oh, I need to go. Someone is trying to call me. Let me hang up so that whoever-it-is can call me back."

One day, I took her for a check-up at her doctor's and dropped her off at the door. When I came into the waiting room, I walked over to sign her in.

"I've already signed in," she grandly informed me. I stopped. I did a double take. Mama had never signed in for herself before.

"You signed in all by yourself?" I asked incredulously. She smiled proudly and nodded. Then I clapped my hands excitedly and cheered.

"Yay!!! You're getting to be a *big* girl!" Mama threw back her head and laughed while everyone else eyed us strangely.

They say that daughters eventually become their mothers. I hope so. Mama's life was much easier than mine. I want to turn into Mama.

Now, if I can just get my sister to do my hair every Saturday.

Scotch-Irish Recycling

My brother-in-law, Rodney, the wizard of wisecracks in our family, was sitting at the island in my kitchen, watching as I put away food from a Sunday School get-together.

I pulled out a Styrofoam take-out container and began to fill it with food for a friend who was ailing.

"Ronda," he said in that tone he uses when I'm about to get a lecture about my stupidity on this or that. "Surely, you don't re-use Styrofoam containers."

I stopped dipping green beans and looked at him incredulously. "Of course, I do." I smiled before I returned the volley. "I'm green. I practice recycling."

He rolled his eyes. "That's not recycling, dummy. That's re-using. There's a big difference."

I thought back to all the times I've seen Mama and my grandmothers wash and dry baggies then stack them away neatly for use again.

I fluttered my eyelashes and smiled coquettishly. "I'm Scotch-Irish and this is the way we recycle."

He shook his head in complete disbelief. "I can't believe you do that. That is the *height* of redneck." Coming from an expert on the matter, it must be true. "What would Jeff Foxworthy say? I'm sure he'd get some good material out of it."

That's when I had to laugh. I thought back to a few weeks before when Foxworthy and his precious wife, Gregg, had been at my house for a simple Southern supper. Jeff and Rodney had stood in the kitchen, chatting, while Louise and I put food away. I pulled out a Cool Whip container and poured mashed potatoes in it. I see no reason to throw great storage containers like this away.

Jeff tilted his head to one side and scratched at his ear. "You know, my sister's got a whole matching set of them bowls." He gestured toward the Cool Whip container. "When we eat with her, she uses them for salad bowls."

Great. One professional comedian and one who thinks he's a comedian making fun of my frugal ways. But it is the way of my people. If my mama could use it again, she never threw it out. My grandmother saved loaf bread wrappers and used them for bags. If she was going on a long trip – usually an hour or so – she'd make her up some sausage and biscuits, wrap them in a paper napkin and put them in a loaf bread bag. When she came to visit us for an overnight stay, she brought her clothes in a paper grocery sack.

"You waste too much," Mama said disapprovingly one day as she watched me unload groceries and throw the bags in the trash.

That's really not the truth, especially according to Rodney. When I'm shopping, I often refuse a bag and just carry my purchase out in hand. I save bath water and tote endless gallons outside to water flowers and trees. This I learned from my Scotch-Irish mama who, long before it was cool to be green, toted her dishwater outside in an old metal dishpan and poured it on her roses every morning. Mama used recycled water all her life. She had grown up humble in the mountains where they toted water from the creek and used the cool water to store a "spring box," which kept their milk and butter chilled. She knew the value of water.

I save string, ribbon, bows, and when possible, wrapping paper. I eat leftovers for a week at a time and air conditioning is never turned on before June for I depend heavily on ceiling fans. In the wintertime, I bundle up good and turn the heat down low. From my ancestors, I believe I've learned well.

Are we thrifty or ingenious? Probably a little of both. But if things keep going like they're going, more people are going to wish they had a Scotch-Irish upbringing.

After all, we were the original recyclers.

Mama and The Freezer

Mandatory to my mama's generation was the owner-ship of a deep freezer and a sewing machine. These, remember, were people who believed in self-reliance and independence. You grew what you ate, you froze or canned it and you sewed what you wore.

To demonstrate my mama's solemn oath to independence, she owned two sewing machines and two freezers.

"Why?" I once asked.

"Because if one gives out, I got a back-up."

Of course.

Well, one of the freezers – a good ol' Frigidaire – is well over 50 years old. Sometime, a long time ago, when the white chest freezer began to show extreme signs of rust, Mama spray painted it black. Then, when the black began to rust, she took blue gingham-checked contact paper and pasted it all around the body. Mama was thrifty as well as clever.

"Smartest woman I've ever knowed," Rodney, my brother-in-law, often said.

The ugly freezer called the "old one" sits across the utility room from the "new one" which is young at 40 years old. And the old one still works. Which is the problem.

"Mama, that old freezer is eating up your power," I'd been telling her for two years before she died. "What do you need two freezers for?"

"What about if hard times come and I need somethin' to eat?" She set her jaw and that's when I knew she would die with two freezers, which, of course, is exactly what she did.

Now, I'm almost as thrifty as Mama though not to the extreme where I go to a restaurant and take home all the free bread they'll give me. Still, when the power bill at Mama's house became my responsibility to pay, that's when I became very interested in the electricity liability of the old freezer.

The day that our electricity bills came and mine was one dollar cheaper than Mama's was the day I decided something had to be done. After all, my house is twice as big as Mama's and I actually live there. Mama's house was empty.

"I'm cleaning out that old freezer and unplugging it," I told my sister. "What's good – I'll move into the new freezer."

First of all, Mama apparently never threw out a margarine tub. Instead, she cooked something, put it in the tub and put it in the freezer. You wouldn't want a perfectly good butter tub to go to waste, would you? She marked everything by putting a piece of masking tape across the lid and identifying it with: Fried Squash, '01. I found many tubs and freezer bags that had been in there for 10 to 15 years.

Good heavens, you have never seen so many containers of homemade vegetable soup and collard greens. If I had five dollars for every package I found, I could pay Mama's power bill for years.

Why do you suppose, I asked myself, she didn't eat some of this soup or collard greens instead of always making fresh batches and putting them in the freezer?

The answer is simple. Mama was a child of the Great Depression, an economic downturn that had nearly smothered the Southern mountains. She had known hard times and wanted to make sure she always had something to eat, even if it was 15 years old.

But you got to hand it to that old Frigidaire freezer. It's outlived five stoves, four washing machines, three microwaves and two refrigerators. Plus, who knows how much longer it'll continue to run. I wonder if the Frigidaire folks have a museum and would like to have it back.

After all, with its gingham checked contact paper decoration over black spray paint, it would certainly be the most unique one in their collection.

And it still works.

The Great Flood

When one of life's tribulations smacked me in the eye, I did not cry. I thought, instead, of Daddy's words from way back then.

I stood among the rubble, stunned by the devastation that my eyes beheld, and heard his words so strong and clear.

"Let me tell you something, little girl," he had said, looking square into my 16-year-old eyes. "Worry not over what hard work and money can replace."

My 16-year-old ears had been grateful for those words at that time. I had been leaving the Sears parking lot, when

I bumped the family sedan into the rear quarter panel of another car. I was beside myself, scared of Daddy's reaction. A few minutes later, he pulled up in his truck, unfolded himself from the cab and sauntered over. I ran to him, sobbing.

"Oh Daddy, I'm sorry!" I blubbered. He was unperturbed. He looked at the minor damage, put his arm around me then uttered the wisdom that would become a mainstay of comfort to me over the years that followed. He took out a pen and piece of paper and wrote a note including his phone number and placed it under the window shield.

"My daughter backed into your car. Call me and I'll fix it."

The lady later called and said, "Thank you so much for leaving that note. Some people wouldn't have."

But not Daddy. He always did what was right and he often spoke rightly, much of it his own self-composed wisdom.

"Worry not over what hard work and money can replace," I heard him instruct as I looked as the mess, the remnant of what was my office and what had been the house that Daddy built, much of it with his own hands, 50 years ago.

I took a deep breath then smiled heavenward. "You're right, Daddy."

When Mama died, I bought the little brick bungalow to use as my office. While I had been traveling hither and yon, a water line in the ceiling had broken. Utter rubble lay at my feet. The ceilings in two rooms had fallen and the water throughout the house was deep enough that Dixie Dew, my dachshund, was learning to swim for the first time. She pulled up one wet paw and looked askance at me.

"I know," I mumbled. "You need your rain coat. But who knew this is what we'd find?"

After a moment of shock, I set into recovery mode. The world's best neighbor, Doug, arrived to turn off the water at the meter then friends Mike, Jon and Brandon showed up.

"I heard there was a damsel in distress," Mike announced in a long, country drawl when he walked in. "And I have come to rescue her." Ankle deep in water, crumbled dry wall and scattered insulation, I found so much humor in his words and delivery that I bent over double with laughter.

"You should rename this place, Noah's House," Karen offered.

For some reason I didn't find that as funny as Mike's comment. But, still, Daddy's words reached across the years and the great eternal divide to guide me. I fretted not over the wood floors recently installed or the newly painted walls bubbling with water. All of that could be replaced with money and hard work.

Then I panicked. The water had poured down on an antique desk and what was in it could not be replaced. There was a Valentine that I had mailed Mama back in 1987. I had created the card and written a poem in red ink to express my gratitude for her belief in me. Her tears had washed away the ink in places so she had inked the words back in.

It was a week before the swollen drawers eased enough to open but there, in a little plastic bag, was that card, perfectly preserved.

Nothing else mattered.

A Long Line of Know-it-Alls

I come from a long line of know-it-alls. Honestly, on both sides of my family, we can pretty much tell you anything you need to know for we know it all. Or so we believe.

Mama was Queen Know-It-All when she was alive. She was so good that you could count on her for any kind of medical or legal advice you needed – her doctoring book was always nearby – and if you were adventurous enough, she'd be happy to tell you how the IRS felt about this or that.

"Okay, Dr. Granny," I'd say to her. "It's one thing to take your advice on spastic colons but if you don't mind, I'd prefer to take my advice on matters of Uncle Sam from paid professionals."

"Well, I could save you some money if you'd listen to me," she'd retort. "But go ahead and throw away your money. I'm just trying to help."

Once, my brother was foolish enough to take some legal advice from her. Let's just say that it did not end well.

Mama was always self-diagnosing herself. "I've got a swimmy head," she said. "It's vertigo."

I'd fold my arms and look askance at her. "And you know that how?"

"'Cause I looked it up in my doctor's book. I got all the symptoms."

Another time she diagnosed herself with pneumonia. "Oh, you do not have pneumonia," I protested from the foot of her bed where she was lying with the blanket pulled up to her chin. "I was just here four hours ago and you were perfectly fine."

She jutted her chin out stubbornly. "I don't care if you believe it or not but I'm a sick woman. I've got pneumonia. I might die with it before night falls."

"Okay, get up, we're going to the emergency clinic." 'Just in case' was what I was thinking to myself.

An hour later, a doctor listened to her chest as she heaved in and out then took a gander at the X-ray. "You've got pneumonia," he announced plainly, unaware of the hammer he had just dropped on my head.

Miss-Too-Sick-To-Live-Until-The-Sun-Went-Down pulled her shoulders back, cocked her head and grinned happily. She pointed an authoritative crooked finger in my direction. "I told you. Don't underestimate my doctoring skills."

My Uncle Delbert, God rest his soul, gave us advice on everything from planting gardens to upset stomachs, to surgery. He believed mightily in the restorative powers of Sea Breeze and the healing powers of ginger and red pepper.

"Red pepper is the best thing in the world for you," he'd say time and time again. "Put it on everything you eat."

Now, I have my own tussle with being a know-it-all. Like Mama, I give advice on things for which I have no expertise. Like raising children. Now, in reality, I know nothing about raising children but I have convinced myself that I know something so I share it liberally.

One of my friends says that whenever I begin with "Listen to me carefully," he knows I'm dead serious about what I have to say. I give him advice regularly and, like a good sport, he plays along. He listens intently, asks probing questions and brags on me for knowing so much. Of all the people I advise – either invited or uninvited – he is my favorite. He understands that my lineage is key to the quality of advice I give.

"How do you know that?" he asked the other day when I was recounting the detailed importance of *Snow White and the Seven Dwarfs* to the legacy of the Disney Company.

"I read Walt Disney's account of it."

"You slay me," he said, laughing. "You really are a know-it-all."

"It runs in the family," I replied. "I was born to carry on the tradition."

Rediscovering Mama

It is my strong and abiding philosophy that good springs forth from the midst of whatever bad happens to us. In the recent days that now trail behind me as time spent sweetly, I have luxuriated in the good that came from the water line break that practically demolished my childhood home.

It was shocking to see the devastating damage and all the material possessions lost, many of no value monetarily yet invaluable to my heart. Though I had bought the house to use as my office and though most of Mama's possessions had long been dispersed to family, friends and the Goodwill, much still remained. There was the bedroom suite she had purchased as a new bride, after working three years in the hosiery mill as well as helping her aunt in her boarding house and diligently saving every penny possible. She began her job for a wage of 18 cents an hour and eventually worked up to 25 cents hourly.

"Your daddy said, 'We'll need to buy some furniture so

I'll make arrangements to make payments on it.' We went down to the store and picked out everything it took to furnish our little apartment, and when it came time to settle up with the man, I just took the money out of my purse and paid for it. I had $345 and your daddy had no idea. You could have knocked him down with a feather when I paid the whole bill."

"Why didn't you tell him you had money saved?" I asked.

"I just didn't."

"Why?"

She shrugged. "I didn't want him marryin' me for my money."

I can understand that.

It was the beginning of a successful partnership, financial and otherwise. Daddy labored to make the ends meet but Mama kept them tied. In a hard knot.

Also severely damaged was a prized, hand-made antique china cabinet that Daddy bought on the one and only vacation we ever took. We had traveled to West Virginia and southern Pennsylvania for two weeks to visit Daddy's sister. While there, he bought it from her next door neighbors, whose Italian grandfather was the superb craftsman on the cabinet, and had it shipped home.

The sofa that Mama bought two months before her final goodbye, the one she was so proud of, was soaked beyond use. And the little desk that, for over sixty years, had held our family treasures and odds and ends including photos and letters, was completely destroyed. Sadly, there would be no saving it. Ironically, it had been one of the few pieces of furniture that I had strongly wanted from Mama's estate. I can still hear her saying whenever I was looking for something, "It's in yonder in the desk."

The insurance company, without complaint or balk, did whatever necessary to aid in making things right, though nothing would be the same again. It took two weeks of drying out with multiple, massive machines before construction could begin. Once the water was dried up, professional movers came in, packed up all things personal and professional and stored them in mobile units moved into the front yard.

After five months, it was time to move back in and un-pack. I began the process as one usually does with these type tasks – resolutely but not enthusiastically. The process took me away from other obligations as well as work that provides wages. It started out as a mundane task but turned into something of extraordinary value. To my surprise, it became a journey of sweetness and discovery, one I shall chronicle for you in the weeks that lie ahead.

As I rummaged among the boxes, I found stories that will speak to many of you. What surprised me most was not what I found of Mama in the remnants that remained of her life.

It was what I found of myself that was the most eye-opening.

The Duct Tape Chronicles

In digging through the material remains of what I con-sider to be my heart's one and only home, I have smiled re-peatedly, even chuckled out loud on occasion, at Mama's thriftiness.

Some might call the evidence of what I have found

"stinginess." A few would say she was being a good steward of whatever dollars she scrounged together. Those of her own ilk – the Scotch-Irish – would say either that she did them proud or admit that she was a bit "quare." That's what the eccentric Scotch-Irish call each other when they think one of 'em is odder than the rest.

Saving money was a full-time occupation for Mama. I found plastic baggies with pennies, a coin purse with nickels and dimes and, behind the mustard and ketchup in the refrigerator, a slotted piece of cardboard with six quarters stuck in it. For some reason, it had been cut in half so I have no idea where the other six quarters went. I'm sure, though, she didn't spend them.

"Watch your pennies and your dollars will take care of themselves," she preached often to me. As I found pennies stuck here and there, I saw myself in the reflection of Mr. Lincoln. I watch cashiers as they ring up my purchases and scour receipts before I leave the counter. I will question an item that is a penny more and demand that I be given the correct price. It's not pretty behavior, I admit. But it's obvious from whom I inherited it.

One particularly parsimonious habit I did not inherit from Mama was her lifelong devotion to duct tape. That wide, silver-colored, strong tape was Mama's most faithful companion. It is possible, from what I unearthed, that she was addicted to it. Apparently, she looked for places to use it.

As the movers were packing up the house to put things in storage during the reconstruction, I was going through drawers and sorting papers. Melissa, the sweet young woman assigned to pack, held up an old kitchen cutting board that had split right down the middle. It was held together by a wide band of duct tape around the center.

"Throw this away, right?" she asked as she dangled the sad looking piece of wood over the trash can.

I chuckled and shook my head. "No. Keep it. Let it not ever be forgot that a woman that frugal once lived."

She shrugged, not understanding, but then wrapped it carefully in bubble wrap and packed it away. Since Melissa packed up the kitchen, I was not aware of all the duct tape first aid until I began to unpack.

The gauge on her pressure canner was mended with several pieces of it. For the record, that's one thing I wouldn't want to be making do with. Pressure canners and cookers unnerve me.

The screens around all her windows were duct taped for heat efficiency and bug control. A chair with the leg broken from it had been glued back then bandaged with tape. Her batter-splattered recipe for chocolate cake had ripped so it was taped back together with duct tape. Apparently, she saw no reason to invest in transparent tape.

Myriad other items had been repaired with the silvery piece of wonder including knives, dishes, lamps, picture frames, loose covers of books, ice trays, vacuum cleaner cords and vases. The bottom of an old, red Folgers tin can had duct tape all around. I don't know why because it wasn't broken. Maybe she was having duct tape withdrawals one day and just had to tape something. I took it home to my kitchen to use. I now open fresh coffee grounds and pour them into Mama's homemade can.

In fact, just like Mama, I threw none of it away. As I said earlier: That kind of frugality should never be forgotten. It should be honored.

Ingenious Mama

Mama wasn't sentimental. In fact, I never knew of any-one who grew up in the Southern mountains during the Depression who was sentimental. They all said they were trying to forget, not remember.

So, as I continued to unpack Mama's belongings after the disaster of a winter's broken water line that destroyed her former home that is now my office, I didn't expect much sentimentality. I, however, am extraordinarily senti-mental. When the contractor pulled down a medicine chest in the bathroom to reveal ancient, pretty wallpaper, I pulled off pieces to save.

Each box, though, reminded me of her uniqueness and the footprint she left on my life. In the sewing room, her Singer machine, so old that it is metal and not plastic, brought to mind the days of my childhood when she had taught me to sew. I remembered my frustration while learn-ing the complexity of putting a zipper in correctly, or my joy when I turned pretty fabric into a lovely dress.

There, as in the kitchen, I found strong evidence of her devotion to squeezing a nickel into a dime. There were end-less bolts of double knit fabric. Remember when? She must have thought that hot, heavy, stretchy knit would make a comeback one day. There were eight irons, seven of which were broken but she had refused to throw any away. My sentimentality did not stretch far enough to keep me from tossing them out, though.

I loved the drawers full of spools of colorful thread she had. And, of course, there were at least a dozen spools onto which she had wound small pieces of thread. She would wind three or four different colored threads onto an empty spool, the lengths only enough to sew on a button or hem a skirt. She threw nothing away. I picked up a couple of spools to throw into the trash but I could not.

For I remembered.

See, Mama was part of that prized generation that took whatever they had and made the most of it. She was such a talented seamstress that she could look at a dress in a store window, cut a pattern for it out of newspaper and duplicate it perfectly. When time came for me to go to college, she turned a spare bedroom into a sewing room and started what became a profitable little business.

Her nimble fingers and shrewd business mind paid my way through an expensive, private college, one dress at a time. She made custom clothes for women but she would also buy fabric on clearance and resell it for a profit or make a dress from it and sell it.

I flipped through one of her "sewing books" as she called the composition notebooks that held the measurements for a couple of hundred customers. She listed name, phone number and precise measurements of bust, waist, hips, sleeve, pants and skirt lengths and arms. I laughed recalling that she always measured where the legs meet the torso, just under the buttocks and would say, "That's the problem area on most women. You have to watch out for that."

That little sewing room was pivotal to whom I became. It paid for braces and college degrees, but it taught me other important things. One, that an entrepreneur is simply someone who takes a skill, finds a market niche and keenly understands profit versus loss. Two, that dreams can be stitched together in inventive, out-of-the-box ways; and three, that if you are willing to apply ingenuity and elbow grease, any mountain can be climbed.

Today, I keep similar notebooks as Mama's but mine hold ideas for stories or books and the listing of columns as I send them out to newspapers. I may never be named to a Fortune 500 list. But like Mama, I know how to turn a profit. And that's what counts.

A Quick, Sharp Tongue

My niece, Nicole, was saying the other day how a quick, sharp tongue is built into our DNA and how we need to watch what we say and how we say it.

If you haven't already read between the lines that was her attempt to be subtle and encourage me to watch what I say. Of course, it was a waste of her sweet breath, but I pretended to pay attention and agreed with what she said.

The truth of the matter is that I'm much better than I used to be. Though I watch my tongue a lot more than in previous times, I have decided that it would be professionally irresponsible to watch everything. It would be career suicide, in fact.

Supposing I minded every word that proceeded out of my mouth then you would stop reading me before long. "Used to be interesting," you'd say to your best friend. "But something's missing. It's just not what it used to be."

Nice is boring. A little of it goes a long way. Now, I believe that the world, as a whole, is mean and we should all be kinder. But a little spice sprinkled on our words now and then make them more interesting.

Take Mama, for instance. She was basically a nice person, loved by many. After she died, dozens of women came forth to tell us how Mama was their best friend.

"I could tell her anything," everyone said. "She was my confidant. She gave me the best advice."

We were amazed as to how many folks Mama had served as confidant. Obviously, she kept their secrets because we never knew anything about it. But, still, nice as she was, Mama's mouth was tart and it never said anything that she regretted.

One day, she saw a woman she liked very much. "She's the sweetest thing," Mama always said about Linda. "I just love her to death."

But Mama's love did not spare Linda from Mama's quick, sharp tongue. Mama took her face in her hands once and said, "Linda, you are the prettiest girl." She smiled admiringly. "You have the prettiest face." She paused for a moment. "But I want to tell you something. You don't need to gain any more weight. You're big enough."

To Linda's credit, she belly laughs when she tells that story. It's her favorite 'Mama' anecdote. See? Mama wasn't intentionally mean. She was helpful. At least that's the way she saw it. And since she didn't watch every word she said – she didn't even watch *one* word she said – she was interesting so people are still telling Mama stories.

A couple of years ago, I did a speaking engagement for a bunch of high society women at an exclusive private club in Nashville, where the waiters served in white gloves. It was all far above my raising, though I tried to hold my own. I was sitting next to the hostess, who requested the salt.

Though I never have had formal etiquette training, I somehow knew to pass the salt and pepper together. Not just the salt. When I gestured to hand it to her, she primly replied, "Please place it on the table so that I may pick it up. I am from a very old, elite Southern family and I have been taught proper table manners."

Every face at our table reddened, except mine. I smiled sweetly as I obeyed. "I'm from a very old Southern family, too," I replied, still smiling with deceptive charm. "I'm from ten generations of Southerners, nine of those in Georgia." She nodded stiffly as I continued. "But my people were from the foothills of the Appalachians and they were very poor. They were just happy to *have* salt to pass."

Sometimes a quick, sharp tongue is a girl's best friend.

Reading the Obituaries

Oh, the ironies of life.

My godmother and I were going somewhere one day when she said, "Did you read the obituaries this morning?"

"Yes, I did." I read two newspapers every morning and check the obituaries for national and local deaths.

"Who is being buried at Mount Vernon?" she asked, referring to a local church cemetery.

I proceeded to tell her, with complete recall, who it was, how old he was, where he lived and who his survivors were. What's crazy about this – at least to me – is that I did not know the man nor did I know anyone kin to him. Yet, I could quote the complete obituary.

After I had recited his obituary, I stopped. "Oh my gosh," I said, shaking my head. "I've become Mama!"

Now, when Mama was alive, in the days before her own obituary was written, she was an encyclopedia of obituary knowledge. She spent a good two hours every day, not just reading but *studying* the obituary page. Her daily commentary included observations from the obituaries.

"I didn't know he had been married before. But he had. It listed a child by another wife." Things like that.

We all counted on Mama to read the obits and keep us posted on who died that we knew. Never once in all my life was I able to scoop Mama on an obituary. She stayed on top of her game.

Once, I had a handyman at the house when she called. "Whatta ya doin'?" was her standard greeting when I answered the phone.

"I have someone here, working," I replied, going on to tell what I was having done.

"What's his name?" she asked.

"It doesn't matter because you don't know him," I replied. He lived in another county, one in which I doubt she knew one person.

"Well, I might," she continued. "Who is it?" She persisted until I broke down and told her.

"Jamison Jackson," she repeated. "Jamison Jackson." The wheels of her mind were turning. It began to come to her. "Oh, I know. Someone in that boy's family died last week."

There was no way that I believed, for one minute, that she knew what she was talking about. "Oh, you don't know that."

"Yes, I do," she replied firmly. "I read the obituary and that boy was listed as one of the survivors." She kept turning it over in her mind for a moment or two then she said, "Oh, I know! It was his grandfather."

I chuckled. "You're making that up."

"No, I'm not." She was resolute. I laughed it off and

hung up the phone. I walked into the kitchen where he was and asked – just so I could prove to Mama how crazy she was – "Did your grandfather die last week?"

He stopped what he was doing and turned around to look at me. His eyes widened and his mouth fell open. "*How* did you know *that*?"

Now, I could say that it's journalistic curiosity that keeps me as an avid reader of the death notices. After all, some people's lives are pretty interesting and others, sadly, seem hardly well-lived at all.

I could also say that I read them to stay up on current events and be well informed or that I need to know to whom I should take a casserole.

I could possibly argue that I'm critiquing the obits to determine how much more I need to do in life, in order to have a decent obituary myself. After all, doesn't that cross your mind when you read one who has had stellar accomplishments?

But the truth of the matter is simply this: I inherited a morbid curiosity from my Mama. Now, I'm just carrying on the family tradition.

The Ring

It would never have occurred to me that it would mean as much as it has, never crossed my mind that I would cherish it as I have. I suppose that's what makes it even more meaningful.

Mama wasn't fancy by any stretch of the imagination. A small cake of cornbread and a cold glass of buttermilk often sufficed just fine for her supper, a home grown, juicy tomato thrilled her beyond measure and presents were often wrapped with masking tape. She was sturdy and solid, not fancy or frivolous.

"If I knowed that I'd live long enough to get the use out of it, I'd buy me a new mattress and box springs," she said once about five years before she died. It sums up the woman bred of the mountains that she was – money was not to be squandered and whatever was bought should do you for a long time.

That's why it seems odd, if a person gave too much mind to it, that Mama had three sets of wedding rings in her lifetime. The first one bought back in 1940, when their "I do's" were said, has a diamond that is nothing much more than a speck. Gradually, they got a little bigger. This I know – they were all Daddy's doings because Mama would have kept that first one and lived happily all of her life. She never longed or lusted for expensive things.

The last one, though, she kept for 35 years. It is a round cluster of small diamonds set in yellow gold. When Mama died and Louise collected together her jewelry, she asked, out of the blue, on the Saturday after we had laid her to rest beside Daddy in that country church's cemetery, "Would you like to have this set of rings?"

Tears filled my eyes and I reached out for them. "Oh," I whispered softly for I had never thought of possessing those rings – the cluster and the thin gold band. "Yes. I would love it."

And so from that day forward, I have rarely been without those rings. They bring a comfort to my heart and spirit that words, no matter how grand, cannot describe. Something rather amazing happened, though, when Mama died and her rings moved to reside on my right hand – the sparkle of that ring seemed to multiply significantly.

As though it had been kissed by the lips of an angel.

"Have you noticed how this ring sparkles on my hand?" I asked Louise.

She nodded. "Yes, I have. I don't remember it shining like that on Mama's hand."

Others have mentioned it, too. One day during lunch, my friend, Sue, reached across the table to take my hand.

"Is that your Mama's ring?" she asked. I touched it lovingly with the forefinger of my other hand and nodded.

"I don't remember it having such a sparkle," she commented.

"No one else does, either," I said. "It's like a gift from God, reminding me that Mama is still with me."

"I know what you mean," she replied, explaining that she had had a ring made from a tie tack that had belonged to her son, Jay, who had been one of my best friends in college. A few years after we graduated, he died of a blood disorder with which he had been born. Sue and I stay close, joined by the bond of our mutual love for Jay.

She pointed to a horseshoe-shaped ring studded with small diamonds. Jay was an avid horseman all his life. "This was Jay's and I had it made into a woman's ring from his ring."

"It helps, doesn't it?" I asked.

"Yes," she replied softly. "It helps a lot."

Time marches on and I move further away on earth from those who are gone but closer to them in eternity.

Meanwhile, I am comforted by Mama's sparkle.

Mama Always Said

"Everything's gonna be alright. God has it all right in the palm of His hand."

Mama always had this porcelain plate hanging on a
wall at home. It shows Jesus knocking on a door that
can only be opened from the inside.

When Mama planned on dying

For at least 20 years, maybe 25, Mama planned her homegoing to heaven. Not a week – and sometimes not a day – went by when she did not use her impending date with mortality in some way.

One day, when I had picked her up to go on a weekend trip, we got in a terrible disagreement over, of all things, chicken and dumplings. She was in rare form, so no matter what I said, she sassed back with something.

Finally, I said, "Okay. That's it! This is the last trip we're going on together. The. Last. Trip."

She turned her nose up and pulled the corners of her mouth down then replied, "I'd be ashamed if I were you. What if I died and this really was my last trip with you. You'd feel really bad. What would you say then?" She smiled smugly. Mamas always think they have the upper hand when they use doom and death over their children.

Quick as a noon whistle at a mill, I replied, "Then, I'd say that I'm a prophet."

That didn't end the argument. As I recall, we stayed mad for a day or two before simmering down and moving on. Other than all the times she threatened to up and die just to teach me a lesson – "That'd show you a thing or two, little girl" – she liked to plan out her funeral.

When one preacher didn't show her the proper respect by visiting as he should have, he was marked off the list as a participant in her final goodbye.

"He'll miss that hundred dollars, I guarantee you," she proclaimed.

As I recollect, he neither officiated nor attended. I guess that showed us all a thing or two.

But there are two things, in particular, that I think about often when I think of Mama and her look toward the grave. It was around Thanksgiving, when we were driving past a grocery store and saw a sign that advertised Duke's Mayonnaise "Two for $3." I hit the brakes, pulled in and said, "That's a deal. I've got to run in and get some."

Mama opened her pocketbook and pulled out two crumpled dollar bills. "Here," she pushed them toward me. "Get me a jar. That'll be enough to do me 'til I die."

Three months later when I was cleaning out her refrigerator after her departure from this earthly abode, I pulled out a half-full jar of Duke's. I had to smile. She was right. She had enough to do her until she died and still had half of it left.

About six months before her call to eternity – now, mind you, she was in good, almost robust health – I went in the house one day and found her sitting, as usual, in her favorite recliner, the footrest kicked up on it. In her hands, she was holding an 8x11 photo. She was in her thoughtful pose which was noted when she rested her thumb against her chin and let her forefinger settle on her upper lip while the rest of her fingers sorta' dangled.

"Whatta you doin'?" I asked.

"I'm admirin' this photo that I had made at church for the directory." She turned it toward me. "Ain't that good of me?" She was full of self-admiration and, truthfully, rightly so. She had on a beautiful, deep pink suit, lipstick a shade darker, and her hair, teased to a bountiful fullness by Louise, was perfect.

"Yeah, real pretty."

She held it at arm's length, studying it in all its glory and said, "I had this made so that when I die, y'all can put this in a frame near the casket."

I rolled my eyes and walked to the kitchen.

As it turned out, that's exactly what we did. And it just goes to prove that if you threaten long enough to die, one day, you will.

The First Mother's Day Without Mama

As anyone can attest the first Mother's Day that comes after a mama's death is a tough one. All holidays are that first year until, gradually, life without Mama is a way of life. I will always recall Mama's last Mother's Day on earth with regret and hurt.

Mama had gone to early church with me and then we were planning to eat out. Mama loved to eat out. It was a simple but large joy in her life. A few months before her death, Mama called me up as night was starting to fall. Louise had taken Mama to get her hair done that day and Mama, who was still getting perms to give body to her baby-fine, lifeless hair, was all fixed up.

"Hey," she said. "I have an idea. Let's go out to eat tonight."

I shook my head in disbelief and looked at the clock. It was almost 6:30 p.m. and usually Mama had eaten by then. It was also Tuesday night and not a night that we would just up and go out to eat.

"Huh, tonight?" I was dressed in bumming-around-the-house clothes, no makeup and my hair was pulled back into a ponytail.

On the other end of the phone, you could hear happiness and a light spirit. "Yes. I got my hair done today and it looks so pretty that I don't want to waste it by sitting home. I want to go out." She paused. "I'll buy. Let's go to O'Charley's. I love their chicken fingers."

As I've said before, I knew she was serious when she offered to buy. When we were together, either I took the check or she handed it to me. I didn't want to go. I was wrapping up my day and I didn't want to get dressed, fix my hair and put on makeup. But I knew it was important. Quickly, my brain processed it and said to me, "Don't turn down this opportunity. She rarely calls like this. Do it."

"Well, okay, I'll have to get dressed. I'll be over there in 20 or 30 minutes." I lived just over the creek from Mama.

A bit later, I pulled into the driveway and there she was, waiting on the porch. She got in the car, turned to me with a big smile and said, "See? Don't I look pretty? I think this is the best she's ever done my hair." She smiled brightly. "I just needed to show it off."

Mama was hard to please about food in a restaurant. Occasionally, she said, "It's good" but mostly she said, without enthusiasm, "It's okay" or, with aggravation in her voice, "This ain't fit to eat. If I couldn't cook no better than this, I'd just shut the doors and go home."

On the day that would turn out to be her last time of

Mother's Day celebration, we went to early church as usual and planned on dining out afterwards. Most restaurants were serving brunch so we looked forward to that. But, already, the people were lined out the doors, waiting for seats. I hate to wait at restaurants. I rarely will do it. I'd really rather be hungry than wait. So, at the third restaurant when we pulled in and saw the long line – and it was still half an hour before they opened, I said, "I'm not doing this. I'm not waiting an hour to eat."

Mama was in an unusual reasonable mood. "Whatever you want to do is fine with me. I don't care. We can go home and make a sandwich if you like."

I did a double take and looked at her. She looked at me. "I'll make a pan of biscuits and fix us something. We don't have to go out to eat."

"It's Mother's Day. I hate for you to do that. Let's see if we can find something else." We drove down what is the main drag of restaurants in our hometown when I spotted one that was popular with the locals for its home cooking. There was no line and only a few cars in the parking lot.

"Hey, how about this?" I asked, feeling that we had found the right place. It was the kind of food that Mama liked.

Airily, she waved her hand. "Anything's fine with me."

These were words that I heard come out of Mama's mouth no more than five times in my life. And then it was because she was in an exceedingly good mood and could afford a generosity of spirit. I pulled in the parking lot and we went in to find only seven or eight people eating. Right then and there, I felt something wasn't right because the place was always packed. What we were to discover in the next few minutes was that, unbeknownst to me, the restaurant had changed hands and the people who had run it for 30 years were no longer the owners. We went through the buffet line to discover that the biscuits were hard, the cream gravy was setting up, the eggs were runny, the grits not cooked completely and the bacon was soggy and floppy. I don't remember ever having a worse meal in a restaurant. A Hispanic family had taken over the restaurant and were trying to cook Southern style. This, as you might imagine, was not a good idea. At all.

To my credit, I felt terrible right then and there. It didn't take Mama dying nine months later to bring on the regret. But what made it worse was how incredibly sweet that Mama was about it. It was completely out of character.

"Mama, I'm so sorry. I didn't know that Johnny had sold this restaurant. This is awful."

She shook her head as she chewed on a tough biscuit. "This is fine. Anything's good with me. I don't mind at all." Trust me when I say this was not the woman I knew.

"But it's terrible."

"No it's not. It's fine. I'm just glad to get to eat out and not have to cook."

I'll die with this sadness, knowing that my impatience resulted in a perfectly lousy final Mother's Day for Mama. I think about it every time I drive pass that deserted building (the restaurant was out of business within two months, proving just how bad it was) and I think about it every Mother's Day and feel a tinge of sorrow in my heart. When the next Mother's Day came and Mama was in heaven, I used her own words to write the Mother's Day column.

Needless to say, I sobbed all the way through it as I wrote it and as I edited it.

Mama Has Her Say, Finally

For a couple of years, I had been trying to get Mama to write my column one week. Well aware of how much readers loved her, I knew they would be tickled to get her side of our story.

"It's only fair," I told her the first time I brought the subject up. "You should have your say." I smiled. "It's the journalistically-balanced thing to do."

A look of delicious mischief spread across her face. She grinned delightedly. "Really?" That look made me a little nervous but I swallowed hard and stood my ground.

"Of course."

She arched one eyebrow and studied me for a second, her mind obviously turning. I was getting more nervous, the saliva was dissipating from my mouth. Slowly, she nodded and then chuckled. "Okay, little girl. I'm gonna do it." She winked. "You just wait."

Though I was a bit apprehensive over what she might say, I knew she would produce a highly entertaining column. Mama had a way with words as both a storyteller and a writer. I had no doubt that she could handle the task. That's why I stayed after her.

During Thanksgiving, we discussed it at greater length and she was growing more excited about it. She mentioned a couple of stories about me that she was thinking of telling. I vetoed them immediately.

"No, you're not," I replied emphatically.

She grinned. "Look at the stories you tell about me."

"Look at the stories I *don't* tell about you," I countered. "There are some things that can never leave the confines of this family."

A few weeks before she died, I stopped by to see her one afternoon. She was relaxing in her favorite chair, drinking a cup of coffee. We chatted first about this, then about that and, suddenly, something popped into her head. She lighted up. "Oh I forgot to tell you," she was grinning beatifically. "I have started writin' my column."

"Really?" I chuckled. "That's great."

Teasing mischief danced in her eyes and she pointed that slightly crooked forefinger at me, holding her coffee cup in the other hand. "You just wait, little girl." She laughed. "Your comeuppance is comin'."

Mama died before she finished the column, but a week after her death I found the last words she had written. In her sprawling handwriting, she had penned her words in the composition book she called her "sewing book" because it was where she kept measurements and sewing notes. I held my breath as I read her words and then the tears fell gently down my cheek for she had written:

I have had several people say to me, 'You should write a column about Ronda since she writes so much about you.' So here goes. I will have to say good things about her, I'm sorry to say. I have forgot all the bad things. I remember the good.

My first thought is how blessed we were to have her late in life. She was such a joy. With one in college, two in high school, who would have thought a new baby would bless our home? Bless it, she did. We were all so happy with her.

I called Karen and read the passage to her. "Ronda," she said softly. "That's a gift from the Lord."

Yes, it is. From beyond the grave, Mama had her say. She got in the last word and Lord knows nothing would have pleased her more. To be honest, nothing could please me more, either.

I'm sure this is the only Mother's Day gift I will ever receive but that's okay with me. For once – maybe the only time ever – I am happy to let Mama have the last word.

And the last laugh.

The summer before Mama died, she and her
great-granddaughter, Zoe, spent lots of time together in the
garden, gathering vegetables. I was leaving Mama's
house one day when this sweet scene captured my
fancy, so I grabbed my camera.

Mama takes her leave

The phone rang and I, barely conscious to the dawning of a new morning, lifted my head from the pillow and glanced at the digital clock: 7:15 a.m. "Hello?"

"I'm ready!" Mama's voice rang with merriment, edging close to glee. The previous day had been one of the happiest of her life. She had been the star of a charity fashion show that I had emceed. It's funny, actually it's comforting, to look back and know how gracious the good Lord was and how He supplied my needs before I had a need. Three days earlier, I had been driving on I-85 in the waning daylight toward Montgomery for a press association convention when it occurred to me that Mama had so many fans, many of whom would be attending the fashion show. So, why not have Mama as a surprise guest? The organizers of the fashion show loved the idea and, for some reason, it took no convincing for Mama. She readily agreed.

Usually with Mama, when you wanted her to do something you had to work her and usually it took plenty of work to get her to do something that wasn't her idea in the first place or one that she wasn't set on. But what actually happened was that I hung up with Helen, who was organizing the fashion show, and called Mama.

"I just talked with Helen Hardman about the fashion show on Saturday and we think it would be a great idea if you modeled in it." I braced myself, waiting for a grumbly "no" or a scoff or any amount of opposition to the idea. Mama was rarely easy. Once, Louise and Rodney had tried to convince her to join Rodney's mama, Bedelle, on her weekly trips to the senior center. Now, Bedelle and Bonelle together were a circus act. I could write an entire book on that. Folks still talk about when Louise would take them to the beauty shop together and how they debated and argued with each other. One thing was for sure: If one liked something, the other was bound and determined to despise it. The root of this rivalry probably went back to childhood when Daddy had a crush on the stunningly beautiful Bedelle, who would grow up to become a county-wide beauty queen. Once, Daddy had given her his Baby Ruth candy bar to prove his love. He was 11. Bedelle never let Bonelle forget that until one day while at Sunday dinner at Louise and Rodney's, Mama held up her hand and said, "Now, Bedelle, I've heard enough about the Baby Ruth candy bar. Ralph is dead and gone and I don't want to hear another word about it." Bedelle opened her mouth to say something and Mama stopped her, "I mean it, Bedelle. Not another word."

Bedelle, or Mama B as she was called by everyone throughout the country, loved her days at the seniors' center. That meant that Bonelle was having no part in it. As Rodney tried to convince her of how much she would enjoy it, Mama folded her arms and set her jaw.

"I ain't goin'. I don't care nothin' about it," she said.

"Well, Bonelle, you'd have lots of fun," Rodney continued.

Mama glared at him. "I don't like fun."

I figured that Mama would see a fashion show as fun and would want no part of it. I braced myself for the argument. Instead, I heard this girlish giggle and Mama said, "Ronda, you don't mean it. They want an old woman like me to model in the fashion show? Me?"

I overcame my moment of stunned silence to say, "Yes! Mama, you're a star and they want all your fans to see you."

You would have thought that Mama had been chosen by David O. Selznick to play the coveted part of Scarlett O'Hara in *Gone With The Wind*. She was beside herself with joy and excited anticipation.

The next day, unannounced, she strolled toward the stage, modeling a gray coat, black pants and a pink scarf around her neck. I walked over, took her hand, helped her up the four steps then turned to the audience. "Ladies, meet Mama."

Four hundred women broke into applause and cheers. They had read long and often of Mama's escapades and many had longed to meet her. The entire audience jumped to its feet for a three-minute-long standing ovation. The response thrilled her and tickled me. We hugged each other and, laughing together, we addressed the audience. One of the attendees was Kristen Magnum, a reporter at the *White County News*, who captured the moment on camera. It would become the most precious photo in my collection and is the one at the beginning of this book. The last photo taken of Mama and me.

Mama deserved the happiness she had that day. When we got in the car to start home, she was still beaming. "I have had the best time. This has been one of the most wonderful days of my life." She was holding a bouquet of flowers that Louise had given her. She turned and said, "I'm not ready for it to end. Let's go out and get somethin' to eat. Can we do that?"

"Absolutely."

All through dinner, she chatted happily about the fuss that everyone had made over her and what this one or that one said. On the drive home, she talked about what a perfect life she had had.

"I got everything I ever wanted in life. A wonderful husband and children. No one has ever had a better life than me. You know that?"

My heart was so joyous to see the light radiating from her face. The last several weeks had been sad and hard. She had struggled but always said, "I'm holdin' to the mighty hand of God. He won't let me down."

Eight weeks before, in early December, I had cleaned up my house and dressed. It was 11 a.m. and I was in a wonderful mood because I was preparing to sit down and work on a new book. It can be challenging to make a living as a writer because so much gets in the way daily to keep me from writing. The phone rang and the caller I.D. said it was Mama.

"Hellooooo," I said cheerfully.

"Ronda, I need you to come over here." She was perfectly calm but somber. My heart sped up.

"Mama, what's wrong? Are you okay?" Panic started to flood me.

"I'm fine," she said. "I just need you to come over here because I need to tell you something."

It was bad. I just had the feeling. I threw down the phone and ran out the door. I was wearing a brightly colored, striped turtleneck sweater, jeans and my warm house slippers. I jumped into the car and roared out of the driveway. In less than a minute, I went from my bedroom to Mama's kitchen. I got there so fast that when I ran in, Mama's hand was still on the receiver of the phone that hung on the wall. Collected and calm, she looked at me.

"Mama, what is it? Is it Uncle A.J.?" I asked, referring to her brother who was very sick.

"No. It's Randall."

My brother? "What happened? Is he sick?" He had been struggling for a couple of years after a kidney infection had gone septic and taken him to the brink of death.

"Worse." Her lower lip trembled a bit. She looked me squarely in the eye. "He's dead."

I clutched my heart and my knees buckled. For only a second. Then I jumped up and ran to her. He had suffered a massive stroke. I threw my arms around her. "Mama, are you all right?" She loved my brother. She babied him. We always claimed that he was her favorite which, a few times, she bothered to deny.

In my life I have known sorrow and grief, but the greatest I ever lived through was watching my mama suffer over the loss of a child. This I have come to know: The deepest sorrow known to humanity is a mother who loses a child that she birthed. After I called my sister, Mama, stunned, sank down into her favorite recliner. I pulled up a footstool and rubbed her knees. She held her hands to her face and began to howl in loud sobs, crying, "Dear Lord, please help me." I could do little but watch.

Mama was a trooper, though. She was raised of the mountains. She was stoic. She pulled herself together and, bravely, she carried on with emotional restraint after that first big cry. A week later, she was diagnosed with pneumo-

nia. I feared she would just give up and die. Though weak
and emotionally drained, she fought and, by New Year's,
had recovered. She had moments or days of sadness but
she, always strong and always dependent upon the Holy
Spirit, refused to succumb. A great-grandbaby was born
and she said, "This is the circle of life. One goes and one
comes." When Daddy died a few months later, their first
great-grandchild was born.

After Randall's death, her pen pal, Mary Jo, returned
to me a handwritten note Mama had sent her after her recovery from pneumonia.

*"Death has caused a void in my heart which can never be
filled," Mama wrote. "Continue to pray for me. Prayer is what
has got me this far. I do have a lot of faith. I know God knows
best and one day I'll go to be with Ralph and Randall."*

Mama never questioned God and she loved Him as
much in the trying times as she loved Him in the days of
joy. It is a remarkable legacy to leave for your children and
your children's children.

For all the days I live, I will continue to thank God for
the happiness of Mama's last day on earth and for that
photo that shows the pure joy in her face and mine. When
the phone rang just after seven on that Sunday morning,
she was still on a high from the success and adoration of
the previous day.

"I'm ready! Are we going to early church?"

Early service at the church where we sat with Sims and
Mr. Turnkey began at 8:30 a.m. At my sister's church, it
started at 9 a.m.

"Why don't we go to Louise's and Rodney's today?" She
agreed – mainly because she knew what I didn't at that moment: that Mr. Turnkey was home sick with the flu. That's

another thank you to God Almighty. Mama was at church with Louise, as well as with me, for her final Sunday. When Mama flounced into the church, dressed in the clothes she had worn at the fashion show because she had bought them "since they look so good on me and everybody can't get over how good I look," Louise was standing in the choir, shaking her head with amusement. Mama carried herself with the self-assurance of a star. In the column that follows, you will read my final goodbye to Mama when I shared her homegoing with my readers.

There is much more I could tell you, such as I had to wait in the drive for her on both Saturday and Sunday – even honking the horn, something so unusual for her that it felt like a harbinger of some kind; or that she had arrived at my house for Dixie Dew's birthday party with Louise and her grandbaby, Tripp, and was still reeling with happiness; or how she had stood in the foyer, looking with Louise over photos that set on a table including one of me as a baby and how Louise allowed that it was *she* that truly raised me and how Mama had laughed merrily, flinging that crooked forefinger toward me for the final time and uttering her last words, "That's right. And don't you forget it." I could write about how I laughed and started to turn toward the kitchen when I saw Mama swaying backwards and reaching to grab Louise from behind, how she hit the floor with a thunderous bang, how Louise screamed in anguish while I ran to dial 911.

But what I really want you to know – and what Mama would want you to hear – is that the Lord had mercifully taken her hand and led to cross the River Jordan before she ever hit the floor, and how her last breath in this life was followed by her first breath in everlasting eternity with

Jesus. That's important. Mama was ready to meet her maker and Lord, so she didn't need a long goodbye or a deathbed conversion. She was ready when He called. She would want you to have the same assurance, trusting in Jesus as your Lord and Savior and knowing firsthand that "in a twinkling of an eye," this life can end.

At her funeral, I quoted from Martin Luther King, Jr's funeral sermon for the little girls killed in the bombing of a Birmingham church. "Death is not a period that ends the great sentence of life…..but an open door that leads man into life eternal."

Mama was worried, since the newspaper charged per word, how much her obit was going to cost and had instructed that hers should say only, "I Died." But she needn't have worried because her death was a news story carried – for free – in newspapers across the South. "Mama Dies" read the headline in one because people knew who "Mama" was. The following is the column I wrote when she died. Mama never wrote a book; but she did become a one-name celebrity.

Saying Good-bye To Mama

After early church and Sunday School, Mama and I had hurried to the grocery store. An older friend was ailing badly with the flu, so I told Mama I'd make him some quick homemade chicken soup and she could make the cornbread muffins. Then, I'd run it over to him.

On the way back from his house, I called Mama. "You need to come over to my house and help me get ready for Dixie Dew's party. This soup-making has put me behind."

Dew's seventh birthday party was that afternoon. I always had a birthday party for my sweet dachshund. On my way to pick her up, Mama called. "Don't come right now. Some friends just walked in to visit. I'll call you when they leave."

Two hours later – a few minutes before the party was to start – Mama called back and asked cheerfully, "Have I missed the party?"

"No, but you missed the work," I replied dryly.

She laughed. "Well, that's okay. Just as long as I don't miss the party."

Mama never wanted to miss a party.

I called my sister who was en route and asked her to pick Mama up. A few minutes later, they arrived. Mama was in an exceedingly good mood. The day prior, I had emceed a charity fashion show and she had been the star model. When I said to 400 ladies, "Meet Mama," they went nuts. She was thrilled.

"I've had a ball," she said when we left the event.

A few minutes after she came in my house on Sunday afternoon, we were laughing about something. She grinned, pointed her finger at me, winked and said, "And don't you forget that."

Then, in a twinkling of an eye, just like the Bible says, she stepped from our presence into the presence of the Lord. An aneurysm burst in her head, she stumbled, fell down the step into my sunken living room, hit her head on an antique trunk that had belonged to her uncle and Mama, the best sport ever, was gone.

Mama was one of the greatest characters that ever rose up out of the rural South because she represented us so well. She was faith-filled, family-focused, feisty, plain-spoken and she always colored life with humor and goodwill. Among the many things I will miss is the rapid-fire, enchantingly funny banter we had. She gave retorts well and she took 'em well.

I always thought that when Mama died, that Mama, the character, would die as well in my stories and books. That once she journeyed home, I would write only sparingly of her. But now I know better. Thanks to the outpouring of response from readers who can't bear the thought of life without Mama stories, I know that these stories must go on so I will continue to tell them. For great Southern characters never die. They live forever in the stories we tell and re-tell. Due to columns that have already been delivered to your newspaper, you may read columns in the next few weeks that were written before Mama died. Please cherish them. She loved every word I ever wrote about her and had already read all of these columns.

Be assured that Mama's story has not ended.

Mama, thanks to her salvation, has stepped from this world into life everlasting. Now, Mama, thanks to her star power as a great Southern character, will do what few people are ever able to obtain: She will live eternally both here on earth and in heaven.

She left Dew's party abruptly for a grander, more glorious party. One I've already RSVP'ed for myself, so I'll be seeing her again. As one friend said, "Wow. What a way to go. She modeled in a fashion show the day before then was on her way to a party when the good Lord called."

Yeah, but I just wish she could have stayed at our party longer.

In closing, I'll admit that I miss Mama almost every day. I still shake my head in disbelief over a few of her doings, laugh at some of her sayings and practice many of her teachings. Whenever I'm troubled, I say aloud what Mama always said to soothe me, "It'll be all right. God has it all right in the palm of His hand." And I feel immediately better.

When Mama died, the circle of life continued, but this time it wasn't "one goes, one comes." Six months after Mama died, my niece, Nicole, gave birth to twin girls, one who carries Mama's maiden name, Miller, as her middle name. I guess God decided it would take two to replace Mama. And, knowing Mama, that made her real happy, too.

I can hear her telling Jesus, "They've had a hard row to hoe without having Mama to do for them. Mark my words on that."

Mama Always Said

"You can judge a person pretty good
by the kind of wash they have hanging
on their clothes line."

Acknowledgements

On the day before Mama died, we were in attendance at a fashion show when someone, declaring to be an outraged friend, showed me an editorial letter in one of the newspapers that runs my weekly column. It was a severe letter by a reader chastising me for the stories I told about Mama. She claimed I was too hard and disrespectful.

I was crushed. I loved my mama beyond measure and never meant for my words to sound harsh to anyone. As I stood there, absorbing the reader's unkind declarations, Mama walked up. I showed it to her, so she read the letter then tossed back her head and turned her nose up. Her words were firm. "That woman, whoever she is, needs to stay outta *my* business. I'm fine with what you write about me. I love that you tell stories about Mama and that you made me a celebrity." She beamed.

Thank the good Lord that I read the letter before Mama died and that she soothed my feelings. Otherwise, it could have been a tremendous burden to carry with me until the day of my everlasting eternity. With that said, I must thank Mama. She was always such a good sport.

I am grateful to my faithful readers, my beloved family and to those who have made this book possible including: Jon Rawl, editor, project manager and proofreader; Selena Nix, my niece who is quite an accomplished photographer; Carroll Moore for her design; the *White County News* and Kristen Mangum Cloud for their permissions to reprint the last photo ever taken of Mama and me. Thank you to Lynn Cottrell for enthusiastically allowing use of the photo taken at their ranch and saying, "Your mama was an angel who blessed me." That photo is one of the most precious gifts ever given to me on this earth.

Visit *www.rondarich.com* for other books or information for speaking engagements or email *southswomen@bellsouth.net*.

God bless y'all.

About The Author

Ronda Rich is a best-selling author who writes about the lives of the people throughout the South and shares her stories in speaking engagements with audiences across the country. She is best-known for *What Southern Women Know (That Every Woman Should)*, a classic now in its 40th printing, as well as its two sequels. Her novel, *The Town That Came A-Courtin'*, was made into a television movie starring Lauren Holley and Valerie Harper. "It is my pleasure and privilege to tell stories of the South as only a deeply rooted Southerner can do. Our South is a place well known for its unique language, eccentricities and colorful characters," she says.

Her syndicated weekly newspaper column runs in over 50 newspapers across the Southeast. For the first several years of the column, Mama stories were favorites of her readers. Her career could have ended with Mama's death but the good Lord sent a substitute who is of equal interest to her devoted readers – her husband, Emmy award-winning television writer, John Tinker. His Yankee pedigree goes back as far as Ronda's Southern heritage so the blending of their cultures has proven quite entertaining. The Tinkers make their home on the Rondarosa in the Northeast Georgia foothills of the Appalachians where "Tink" enjoys occasional uncensored use of his chainsaw and Ronda bush hogs the pastures. *www.rondarich.com*